# THINK LIKE

AN INSIGHT INTO HOW 21 OF THE
WORLD'S TOP 21ST CENTURY BUSINESS
LEADERS THINK & WIN

AARON SANSONI

## INTRODUCTION

A HUGE thanks to the 21 entrepreneurs that I've featured in this book, for living a life full of adventure and purpose, giving us all the opportunity to learn and grow from your success. You inspire me daily.

THINK LIKE is an analysis of 21 of the globe's current business leaders and how they think and see the world. Each of these leaders has achieved monumental success in their careers, and, as you'll see throughout the book, their strategies, lessons, principles and actions all impact on the world on a daily basis.

For a long time now I've been obsessed with how the top achievers think, for the simple reason that thought creates action and action creates a result.

Enjoy my take on these phenomenal people and don't forget that there is a difference between reading and learning from this book. Take the time to think after each chapter's final thought. Have your own final thought on what you can learn from that person and what you can apply in your own life and business. I've included a notes page for you after each chapter so feel free to take notes and write down actions you'll take from what you learn. Remember it's only when we take action that we can create a result.

Let me know what you think, and which person you have learned from the most, by connecting using the hashtag #**thinklikebook.** You'll find me across most social media using the handle @aaronsansoni.

Don't forget to keep up to date with our events, programs and training around the globe here: aaronsansoni.com

I'd love to meet you in person and hear your story. Enjoy!

Aaron Sansoni

*Live With Purpose, Live With Passion and Live With Profit!*

# 1

## ELON MUSK

Elon Musk lives in California. Current net worth: US$13.4 billion.

### The solar system is the limit for Elon Musk

Billionaire Elon Musk works on the stuff of dreams: rockets that will land themselves after servicing a space station; the Hyperloop tube that will transport people across the planet at extremely high speeds; an innovative battery that will allow homeowners to store solar power and get off the power grid permanently—after a while it's easy to see why some call him the REAL Tony Stark!

Some of these projects have been criticised, but Musk says, "When Henry Ford made cheap, reliable cars people said, 'Nah, what's wrong with a horse?' That was a huge bet he made, and it worked." Currently, Musk's company Tesla Motors builds electric sports cars.

Musk made a fortune as a founder of PayPal, and he now runs SpaceX, which designs vehicles that take off and travel into outer space—his company has a contract with NASA to send supplies to the International Space Station.

Musk has a clear ability to make money by starting up unique businesses or by getting involved at the ground floor and then cashing in when the businesses have succeeded. For example, Musk started a company called Zip2, an application to help newspapers, with his brother. A salesman by nature, Musk persuaded the directors of the *New York Times* and the *Chicago Tribune* to take on his software. They did, and not long afterwards Compaq bought the business for more than US$307 million—as a result, Musk pocketed a cool US$22 million.

Musk's interest in technology started when he was young. Barely out of primary school, he taught himself programming. At age 12, he wrote an application and sold it, beginning his entrepreneurial career. "I usually describe myself as an engineer; that's basically what I've been doing since I was a kid," he says. He attended high school in South Africa, and later studied computers and economics at universities in both Canada and the United States. He enrolled at Stanford University in California to pursue his studies as a PhD student but lasted only two days before moving into business.

We can learn a great deal about entrepreneurship from Elon Musk. Let's now turn to some of the principles that have made him a success.

## FILLING A HOLE

One of Musk's golden rules is that he only starts a company when it is in a new or emerging field. Even if somebody comes to him with a brilliant idea, if that idea involves starting up a company in an industry that's been around for many years, Musk is not interested. If you are yet to launch your entrepreneurial career, then how confident are you in starting in an emerging field? You must be able to balance the prospects of getting in on a new movement at the ground floor with finding backing or investment for an unproven project. This doesn't mean you have to be an expert on that emerging field. As Musk says, "The odds of me coming into the rocket business, not knowing anything about rockets, not having ever built anything, I mean, I would have to be insane if I thought the odds were in my favour." Nonetheless, he was able to make it work.

## PUT THE CUSTOMER FIRST

It doesn't matter how great an idea is and how enthusiastic you might be, if you lose concentration and leave out the important factors of product quality and customer needs, according to Musk, you're in trouble.

> I'd stay focused on the quality of the product. People get really wrapped up in all sorts of esoteric notions of how to manage etc., [but] I think people should get much more focused on the product

itself—how do you make the product incredibly compelling to a customer—just become maniacally focused on building it better. I think people get distracted from that.

## MOVE BUT DON'T MOVE

Musk talks about the ability of the entrepreneur to change direction without changing direction. By that, Musk means that to pivot in business enables you to switch direction but at the same time keep one foot firmly planted on the ground. Some entrepreneurs think that if their current direction is a failure, it is better to cut their losses and start again. According to Musk, this is not the only option. By all means change direction, but there's no need to 'throw the baby out with the bathwater' as they say. A classic example is X.com. X.com was an online bank that Musk turned into PayPal, now a popular system for making payments online around the world. As he puts it, "Some people don't like change, but you need to embrace change if the alternative is disaster."

## ALWAYS HAVE A PLAN B

One of Musk's interesting characteristics is that he is involved in a wide variety of businesses. Some entrepreneurs concentrate on just one industry or one business, while others have their fingers in dozens of pies. Musk is in the latter category. He has not been afraid to walk away from a business in order to increase his involvement in another. And by walk away, I mean sell. Musk has always sold extremely well. He was only 28 years old when he sold Zip2. Being able to walk away from PayPal allowed him to turn his attention to electric cars, solar panels and outer-space travel.

## WHAT DO YOU DO WITH YOUR PROFITS?

Musk strongly believes that money made should immediately be invested in something brand new. For example, out of the US$22 million he made from the sale of Zip2, he invested US$10 million—almost half—into X.com. Likewise, when he sold PayPal for US$165 million, he invested US$100 million to create SpaceX. Reinvesting in the next venture when one works well is Musk's advice.

## MEASURE TWICE, CUT ONCE

It's a bit of advice for anyone doing some home carpentry, but the principle applies when hiring and firing people as well. Musk believes you should not be in a hurry to expand. That's not to say that you shouldn't look to expand, but warns against doing so too quickly. And when it comes to staff members, Musk advises that one should be slow to hire and quick to fire.

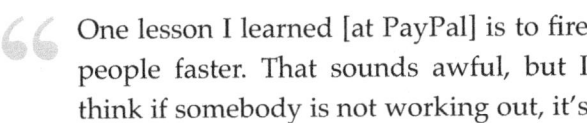

> One lesson I learned [at PayPal] is to fire people faster. That sounds awful, but I think if somebody is not working out, it's

best to part ways sooner rather than later. It's a mistake to try too hard to make something work that really couldn't work.

## BE YOUR BEST CUSTOMER

Are you an enthusiastic advocate of the products you make or the services you provide? Would you really enjoy being a customer of your own company? If your answer is yes, then you are a walking advertisement for your business. As the owner of Telsa, Musk planned to drive his five sons from Los Angeles to New York with only nine hours spent on recharging the electric car's battery. It's a great adventure and great publicity for his company.

It's also about being congruent with what you say —if you're in health and fitness you better be healthy; if you sell a certain type of car, drive it.

## ARE YOU BEING TOO SAFE?

Musk has an interesting opinion on business and business decisions. He thinks that the good business decisions are usually safe, but the great business decisions always contain some element of risk. "If something's important enough, you should try. Even if the probable outcome is failure," he says.

Musk has always invested time and money into emerging, risky industries. Interestingly, Musk went into each of these business propositions knowing that failure was probable. Is it possible that you are playing it too safe? When he first became involved in sending rockets into space, he factored in the option of failure by allowing for at least three launches. Is failure an important part of being creative? If somebody on your team comes to you with an idea, are you willing to work on that idea and encourage people despite the fact that there is an element of risk? If you are not in that frame of mind, then you will not get people coming to you with ideas.

## HOW STRONG A LEADER ARE YOU?

The space project failed twice. When the third rocket blasted off into space, it too failed. There were hundreds of employees working for SpaceX. Surely that was three strikes and you're out? But Musk was determined. He spoke to his fellow workers and said, "For my part, I will never give up and I mean never."

The leader carries not just the financial muscle but is also, in a sense, a spiritual leader. After that speech, Musk's employees agreed that they would do anything for their CEO. Do you have that ability to inspire your people and breed extreme loyalty to you and your business?

Leadership is essential for entrepreneurs, of themselves, their team and their customers—we need to be influencers and persuaders with a vision people can hold on to.

## DO YOU HAVE WHAT IT TAKES?

Musk is quite clear about any would-be entrepreneur and their interest or desire to start a new company. Musk reckons that hard work and high risk are the two key ingredients of success. If you aren't willing to allow either or both of those things, then go and work for somebody else. If you do become an entrepreneur but are not willing to work really hard and take risks, then you may end up miserable. Musk has some pretty down-to-earth advice.

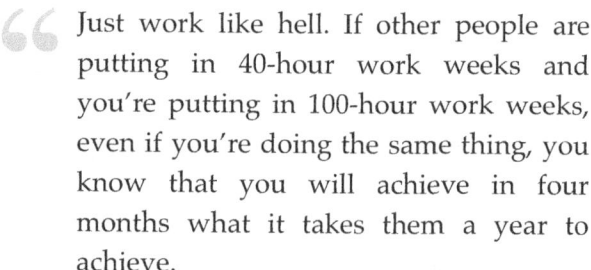

> Just work like hell. If other people are putting in 40-hour work weeks and you're putting in 100-hour work weeks, even if you're doing the same thing, you know that you will achieve in four months what it takes them a year to achieve.

## TAKE A SPIRITUAL PERSPECTIVE

Musk is probably unique in that while he is practical when it comes to starting and running a business, he also looks upon life as being a challenge. It couldn't be better illustrated than in his space-travel activities. Do you have a spiritual perspective on your attitude to work and life? "I think life on Earth must be about more than just solving problems... It's got to be something inspiring, even if it is vicarious," says Musk.

## FINAL THOUGHT

Musk seems to have the Midas touch and has turned almost everything into gold, but he is also very much a human being. He understands the need for hard work. He believes that making tough decisions and being ruthless is an important part of being successful. He knows that in the long run it is better to be tough than to be weak. He is open to new ideas and the fact that he has invested in such a wide variety of industries is proof of his enthusiasm for learning and taking risks.

If the sports racing expression that one should 'make every post a winner' applies to anyone, then it must surely apply to Musk. He took advantage of the opportunity to study. As a teenager, he worked extremely hard at acquiring new skills. He studied for several degrees and made himself aware of business practices and trends. His interest in emerging industries makes him all the more fascinating, leading human civilisation into the wonderful unknown.

But what is most prominent of all his attributes is his constant, unwavering focus on the future we will live in; and creating what we will need for it.

## 2

## SIR RICHARD BRANSON

Sir Richard Branson lives in the British Virgin Islands. Current net worth: US$5.1 billion.

Sir Richard Branson, no virgin in business

Sir Richard Branson dropped out of formal schooling at age 16. Branson suffered from dyslexia and disliked school. His final head teacher famously remarked that he would probably finish in jail or become a millionaire. "I certainly would have failed IQ tests," Branson said. "And it was one of the reasons I left school ... If I'm not interested in something, I don't grasp it." In the end though, the teacher was wrong on both counts: Branson became a billionaire!

Born in 1950 in London, England, Branson is today the head of the Virgin Group, which has control of some 400 companies. The young Branson had an eye for business and for hard work. As a young man, he started a magazine called *Student*. Along with publishing his magazine, he also sold records. Both activities worked together well. With the magazine, he interviewed musicians such as Mick Jagger, and then would sell the records that he promoted in the magazine. This approach was clever for its time.

He moved to selling records from a shop in Oxford Street in the heart of London. Always one with an eye for development, he created his own record label. Branson was writing about music in his magazine, he was selling records that were mentioned in the magazine, and he was running a recording studio so that he could create the records.

Naturally the number of people working for him increased, and because most of the people were beginners in business, somebody suggested they were all business virgins; and so, the name Virgin was born.

Publishing magazines, selling records, and making records were only the beginning of the Branson Empire. He created an airline company and a mobile-phone company, opening these businesses in different countries around the world. Never one to shirk an opportunity, in the early 2000s he created a tourism company with a unique destination: outer space.

Interested in making the world a better place, he turned his attention to investing in research into user-friendly fuels. There seems to be no end to the areas of business he will investigate. He has become involved in entertainment and filmmaking and even in medicine. He is literally a man of many interests, skills, and investments.

Branson is not shy of publicity. When his Formula One team lost a racing bet, he fulfilled his promise to a rival team by dressing as a female air hostess on a flight between Kuala Lumpur and Australia. He is also big on trying to break world records. He's had mixed success with sailing across the oceans or crossing the world in a hot-air balloon. He even appeared in the movie *Around the World in 80 Days* as a hot-air balloon operator.

In politics, Sir Richard Branson has formed and funded an organisation known as The Elders. The idea is that a group of national and international leaders, many of whom are no longer in office, meet to discuss conflicts going on around the world and seek ways to try to resolve them. Branson is a political activist, and will protest and even go on a hunger strike to make his point.

He is interested in the preservation of wildlife, in protecting the environment, and in finding fuels that are less damaging to the planet.

Branson is a strong believer that you can achieve great things regardless of your age. He made his start in the business world at age 16, and now in his 60s, he continues to keep fit and attempts to break records. To Branson, age is a number and not a barrier.

I recall co-headlining with Sir Richard Branson at an event, teaching a huge audience of entrepreneurs in Australia, and was again reminded of his sheer dominance in the 'entrepreneurial game'. He is not showing signs of slowing at age 65!

Let's now look at some principles in Branson's work.

## GIVE A LITTLE TO GET A LITTLE

Branson purchased a stately building and converted part of it into a recording studio even though he had little to no ability as a record producer. How could he get himself noticed and get the business up and running? His answer was to give time in his recording studio to Mike Oldfield without charge. Oldfield took advantage of this free offer and recorded a great deal of his own music that was released under the title of *Tubular Bells*. It was a smash hit and the first release for Virgin Records. Branson wasn't paid a cent by Oldfield for the use of the facilities but the goodwill rewards later down the track were fantastic.

## SHOULD YOU COURT CONTROVERSY OR HUMOUR?

The answer to this question depends on what type of controversy and your reason for courting it. Here is an example. There was a punk band in Britain known as the Sex Pistols, infamous for their hard themes and language. Mainstream record companies sacked them, whereupon Sir Richard Branson signed them to Virgin Records. Not long after they were signed, the band broke up, but an enormous amount of publicity was generated by the Sex Pistols, and Virgin Records certainly benefited. Do you shy away from making a controversial or difficult decision just because it is controversial?

Later in his career, when the London Eye tourist attraction (backed by British Airways, or BA) was going far over its scheduled opening date, because they couldn't erect the circular observation wheel, Sir Richard Branson quickly organised for one of his hot-air blimps to park over the top of the London Eye (that was laying on its side!) displaying the writing *"BA Can't Get It Up!"* He hit front pages and nightly news worldwide. Humour undoubtedly led to more revenues across Virgin brands. How could you use humour in marketing? Does that fit into your brand?

## THINK ABOUT DIVERSIFICATION

If there's one thing you can say about the Virgin Group it is that the companies under its umbrella are diverse. Branson has gone into business with mobile phones, transport, finance, cosmetics, movies, and even his own brand of soft drink. "And you know," Branson says, "I've had great fun turning quite a lot of different industries on their head and making sure those industries will never be the same again, because Virgin went in and took them on."

If you have found success in one area of business, why should you not be equally successful or even more so in another area? And does this new area have to be related in any way to the field in which you are currently operating? It certainly doesn't in the hands of Sir Richard Branson. If it can work for him, then can it work for you by taking the essence of what you have created in business and applying it to another industry?

## DO YOU LOVE YOUR BUSINESS?

Sir Richard Branson puts his heart and soul into his business. One of the first things he did when he started out was to create Virgin Records. He turned it into a highly successful business and some 30 years after he created it, he sold it for around US$1 billion to the recording giant EMI. It's reported that upon making the sale Branson cried. Many other entrepreneurs may think that he would be cheering and laughing at such a financial windfall. But he had put his heart and soul into that business, and while he was glad of the financial return, he was sad because it was no longer under his control. Do you have your heart and soul wrapped up in your business?

## IF AT FIRST YOU DON'T SUCCEED

Branson is a big believer in constantly being on the lookout for new projects. He says business opportunities are like buses—there is always another one coming.

Remember, if you try a particular project or venture and it doesn't work, don't be discouraged. Always learn from your failures or mistakes, but also keep a watch because another bus will soon be coming along.

## WHAT TYPE OF BOSS ARE YOU?

Branson has an interesting philosophy on the way the

boss should behave. "I believe in benevolent dictatorship, provided I am the dictator," he says.

Branson seems to have been able to strike that balance. He takes a keen interest in his employees and is even known to write personal letters to individuals. However, he maintains the belief that the boss should also be, in some ways, a dictator. If you are the boss and you are super-sensitive, then you are probably in the wrong job. According to Branson, a leader or a serious entrepreneur is somebody who doesn't worry about criticism or what others think. Branson believes that a true leader makes and takes decisions decisively.

## HOW IMPORTANT IS EDUCATION?

Branson is a strong believer in education from the school of hard knocks. "You don't learn to walk by following rules. You learn by doing and by falling over," he says.

When Branson began his business life by starting a magazine, he had never had a journalism lesson in his life and had no degree. Maybe if you are apprehensive about tackling a particular project, the solution is to drop the apprehension and get stuck into the project. If you wait until you are qualified to do something you may never do it. Yes, you may make mistakes, and many of them. But, as Branson points out, the fastest and best way to learn is by doing.

## BE DIFFERENT

The world is full of entrepreneurs who play it safe. Branson could never be placed in that category. In 2004, he started a new company called Virgin Galactic. This is a tourism company but the destinations are slightly different; with this company, the trips are to outer space. It costs $200,000 for a ticket and so far, more than 400 people have paid and booked. Will it ever take off ? That's not the point. The point here is that Branson is willing to try something different. Is it risky? Of course, it's risky, but by doing something unusual and different and making yourself unique, you certainly gain an enormous amount of publicity.

It is not just in unusual business ventures that Branson shines. It's as if he has a crystal ball and can look into the future. Obviously, there is a huge need for a reduction in the use of oil to power motor cars. Electric or solar-powered cars are alternatives, but so too is the ability to develop gasoline that is far friendlier. The Virgin Green fund is another business started by Branson that looks at ways to improve our lives without damaging the environment. His approach is encapsulated in a book he published entitled *Screw Business as Usual* (a great read).

There are many ways entrepreneurs can improve their performance. They can endeavour to treat their employees better. They can build stronger ties with their community, and they can certainly leave the environment in a better place. "But with extreme wealth comes extreme responsibility," Branson says. "And the responsibility for me is to invest in creating new businesses, create jobs, employ people, and to put money aside to tackle issues where we can make a difference."

## YOU CAN'T SEPARATE WORK FROM PLAY

Branson is a strong believer that you cannot and should not separate your business activities from the rest of your life. The things you do in business impact the way the world operates. According to Branson, you should not only consider the bottom line of your business, but also the impact your business will have on your staff, your community, and the world.

## BE HAPPY IN YOUR OWN SKIN

According to Branson, doing what you want to do is important, but you must be happy to do so. There's little point in making money and being successful if you are frustrated and unhappy. "My general attitude to life is to enjoy every minute of every day. I never do anything with a feeling of, 'Oh God, I've got to do this today'."

## PERSONAL BRAND

Sir Richard Branson has to be one of the absolute best examples of using your personal brand to impact your business brands. From jumping off buildings for company launches, to travelling the globe educating entrepreneurs, to using his name to get joint-venture partners, investors, staff, suppliers and more—he gets everyone wanting to be involved. He understood at an early stage in his empire building that a strong personal brand could have an extremely positive effect on his business success, and never looked back.

What can you do to get yourself known in your target market? Do you have a personal site? Do you market yourself ? Do you have a strategy to get you out there as an expert or authority?

At the end of this book I'll show you how to do this exactly!

## FINAL THOUGHT

It's difficult not to admire Sir Richard Branson. I've certainly placed him as one of my main mentors and was honoured to speak at the same event as him in 2012 and then co-headline an event together with him in 2015 (a big highlight for me).

He was a high-school dropout, yet he worked hard and looked to expand wherever he could. When you think that he started with a small magazine and interviewed musicians, it's truly remarkable that the Virgin Group is now so successful, so widespread, and so open to new ideas and progress.

If as an entrepreneur, you are locked into a single type of business operation or industry, have you given yourself the best opportunity to succeed? Is it possible to apply the talents you've already used in your current situation to other prospects? Could you expand? The example of Branson is a great one to follow. He didn't expand too quickly. He didn't put great financial strain on his business operation. He expanded in logical ways once he had built a brand that people would follow. All of his work has both served the Virgin group of companies and improved greater society. A great example to all us entrepreneurs.

# 3

## JACK MA

Jack Ma lives in China. Current net worth: US$28.6 billion.

From inexperience to domination: Jack Ma's China success

Born in 1964, Jack Ma didn't see his first computer until he was 33 years old. That didn't stop him from creating one of the biggest online businesses of all time. Arguably China's most successful entrepreneur and philanthropist, Ma created a company called the Alibaba Group in 1999, an umbrella organisation for a number of online businesses. Ma works so hard to improve his company because, he says, "if Alibaba cannot become a Microsoft or Wal-Mart, I will regret it for the rest of my life."

Ma says that in his youth he was led to believe that "China was the richest, happiest country in the world. So when I visited Australia, I thought, 'Oh my God, everything is different from what I was told.' Since then, I started to think differently." Ma laughs about the Internet's first arrival in China. The dial up connection was so slow that it took more than three hours for the first page of a website to appear. At the end of the 20th century, Ma saw that there was a huge need for Chinese companies to receive assistance and that the Internet was the way forward.

Let's look at what has made Ma so successful.

## PERSEVERANCE

How many of us have begun our business life with the sorts of handicaps or difficulties faced by Jack Ma? Ma had to overcome a language barrier in order to spread his business around the world. Ma's parents were traditional Chinese storytellers and musicians; nobody in his household spoke English. To learn English, Ma regularly rode his bicycle an hour to a hotel where he conversed in English with foreigners. He persisted, becoming a self-employed guide for English-speaking tourists. He even did this for free, so determined was he to become fluent, because he knew how important this skill was to his success. That's dedication.

One example of his 'if at first you don't succeed then try, try again' attitude came when Ma attempted to gain entry into a teaching institute. He failed the entrance exam twice, but on the third attempt he was successful. In 1988, he graduated with a BA in English. He was so competent that he went on to become a lecturer in English at a Chinese university.

Unsatisfied with his excellent qualifications, Ma

enrolled in a graduate school of business in order to improve his knowledge and skills for a business career. In Ma's case, it certainly helped that he had a passion for learning. If you can capture some of his passion and direct it towards acquiring skills, information, or knowledge in a particular area for your business, the sky is the limit.

## FAILED STARTS

While Ma has proven to be a success, it wasn't always easy. Yet some successes can develop out of initial failures. In 1995, Ma visited the United States for the first time, staying with a family in Seattle. One member of the family was in charge of one of the first American ISPs, giving Ma a firsthand look at what the Internet could do. He was amazed by its potential.

When Ma used a search engine to look for sites in China, he typed in the words *China* and *beer*. How many websites came up? Zero. On the Internet, China was clearly a barren and unexplored market of over a billion people. You can imagine the thoughts going through Ma's mind about the possibilities. Here was an opportunity screaming out for an entrepreneur.

Returning home to China, Ma's first Internet project was to start the equivalent of the Chinese Yellow Pages; however, this failed. Entrepreneurs make mistakes often and have false starts regularly—this was just a learning experience for Ma. Within years from this he had started what became the Alibaba Group.

Ma saw two massive opportunities: the billion plus

population of his homeland, and the burgeoning beast, the Internet. Bringing the two together was the tricky part, but when he eventually did so, his success was outstanding.

Are you looking at new opportunities and prospects for your business? What about new markets? Are there ways you can launch into new areas or further develop what you are operating already? One of the most exciting parts about being an entrepreneur is that your next big discovery is yet to occur. Keep looking!

DEVELOPING RESPONSIBILITY THROUGH EQUITY

Jack Ma organised the ownership of his business in a diversified way. When he started out, he didn't intend to own all of the business. Instead, he understood that loyal associates would work harder to improve the business. "I gathered 18 people in my apartment and spoke to them for two hours about my vision," Ma says. "Everyone put their money on the table, and that got us $60,000 to start Alibaba. I wanted to have a global company, so I chose a global name."

When a high-school student worked part-time for the business, Ma both paid the student fairly and offered equity in the company. So not only were his employees loyal, they were determined to boost the performance of the business too—a brilliant way to retain and inspire your team.

Ma also made a point of being upfront and transparent with his team. There were no private contracts, which meant that everyone knew the pay and bonus structure, along with the equity shares in the group. Part of the key to Ma's success was in hiring people who were talented, of course, but also people who would take responsibility. There is something particularly powerful about a team that is not only enthusiastic and dedicated, but that also seriously wants the business to succeed.

Is this a move you could make? Is there a way that you could share equity in your business with those members of your team who have displayed an excellent and continuous period of service? Or is there another way you can show your gratitude with a reward that will ensure loyalty?

## TAKING ON THE BIG BOYS

When Jack Ma started Alibaba, the main thrust—or rather the only thrust—of the business was dealing with business-to-business vendors. The company was very good at its core business of helping Chinese businesses find success overseas, although it took some time for them to make serious money.

Ma decided to build a second site, this time concentrating on consumers. Most of his executive team thought the idea was crazy, arguing that he should focus on what he did best—helping businesses succeed overseas. Business 101 tells us that taking on too many tasks weakens the whole company.

Undeterred, Ma was determined to broaden the business base of his company so he started TaoBao, a direct competitor to eBay's well-established Chinese partner EachNet. So what did Ma propose? He made sure to differentiate his company from the Chinese eBay through its funding structure. EachNet took a commission on all sales or auctions, so Ma decided his online auction business would not take any commission. A bold and decisive move, it was also a potentially risky one. But if your opponent has a huge lead, you need to take drastic action to get into the game by creating what I call an 'Irresistible Offer', just like Ma did.

The tactics Ma used in this battle involved guerrilla marketing, and resulted in Ma receiving the nickname for which he would become famous. He said, "eBay may be a shark in the ocean but I am a crocodile in the Yangtze River. If we fight in the ocean, we lose—but if we fight in the river, we win." It wasn't long before TaoBao was able to obtain 70% of the Chinese online shopping market. This was a tremendous victory and Ma's nickname stuck: the Yangtze Tiger.

When Ma wrote a book about the beginnings of Alibaba, he said, "I was scrawny when I was younger but I was a terrific fighter. I was never afraid of opponents who were bigger than I." What sort of a fighter are you? Are you prepared to take on the big kids? Are you prepared to make sacrifices and try alternative marketing methods to get market share? Are you ready to back yourself even when the majority are telling you you'll lose? Some of the moves Ma made were unusual, but if you want to be seriously competitive you may need to consider unusual tactics. Even if you lose money at first, an unusual tactic could be the best, or even the only way you can become a profitable and successful entrepreneur. Be bold.

## BE HONEST AND OPEN

One of the fastest ways to fail in any relationship, be it in business or in your personal life, is to be false. A person who is not authentic will quickly be discovered and undone. Jack Ma may be eccentric, but he is honest and open. He has developed a wildly successful business across continents, but even after he became a billionaire and one of the wealthiest people on Earth, he never changed his personality or attitude toward other people. He always believes in putting the customer first and has put that theory into practice throughout his entire life as an entrepreneur.

If you are looking to consolidate your business or to improve it and take it further, make sure that you consider looking inward first. Are you being true to yourself ? Are you being honest and open with your team, your clients and your suppliers? Are you being yourself?

After fifteen years at the head of the Alibaba Group, Jack Ma published his philosophy:

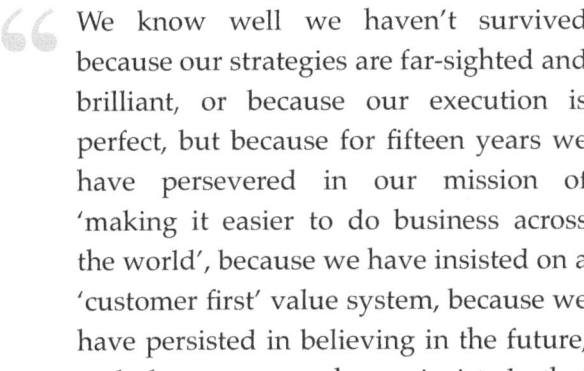
> We know well we haven't survived because our strategies are far-sighted and brilliant, or because our execution is perfect, but because for fifteen years we have persevered in our mission of 'making it easier to do business across the world', because we have insisted on a 'customer first' value system, because we have persisted in believing in the future, and because we have insisted that

normal people can do extraordinary things.

## FINAL THOUGHT

Jack Ma started from scratch—no money, no English skills, no computer knowledge—and yet he went on to become a giant of industry. Probably the most important action taken by Ma was his willingness to offer his work colleagues equity in the company. Sometimes a good idea needs more people with a real reason to push it forward, and maybe even tip in some capital like Ma's team did. Sure, timing was perfect for Alibaba, but Ma's team approach worked.

This reminds me of the saying 'Do you want 100% of nothing or a percentage of something?' Don't be greedy, but choose your equity partners wisely.

Ma also showed the courage to take on the major players in an industry. He saw opportunity and wasn't afraid to challenge the establishment in China. There are so many lessons we can learn from Jack Ma. Which ones can you apply to your business?

# 4

# OPRAH WINFREY

Oprah Winfrey has residences in several US states. Current net worth: US$3 billion.

## Success from within: the lessons of O

Oprah Winfrey, one of the world's richest women, believes material success in business isn't the end game—it's just the starting point for something greater. "What material success does," she says, "is provide you with the ability to concentrate on other things that really matter. And that is being able to make a difference, not only in your own life, but in other people's lives."

Winfrey has certainly influenced the lives of millions of people, and it all began with a talk show out of Chicago, *The Oprah Winfrey Show*. For years, she delved into social issues—not the typical trivial topics of talk shows—and gave gifts to her audience members. She even has her own cable channel called

OWN, or Oprah Winfrey Network, and a magazine simply called *O*, to expand her influence. Not many people know she was an actress before she became a TV host, or that she even worked as a TV newsreader.

People associated with her have certainly seen the benefits of her friendship. *Dr Phil* is a popular TV show on lifestyle and behaviour, which is now one of the biggest in the world, and Phil McGraw got his break by appearing on Winfrey's shows. Winfrey also furthered the career of Mehmet Oz—the famous and controversial TV doctor who advises people on everything from heart conditions to eating right.

One of her special success stories, a story of helping others succeed, is her book club. Envy the author and publisher if Winfrey selected their book. These books almost always became bestsellers overnight and gained worldwide publicity that money literally couldn't buy. The desire to encourage authors and encourage readers to take up books in the Digital Age came from her own experience with the printed page. "Books were my pass to personal freedom," Winfrey says. "I learned to read at age three, and soon discovered there was a whole world to conquer that went beyond our farm in Mississippi."

These examples show that Winfrey's business success comes through encouraging others. Her business advice tends to focus on internal factors—improving yourself, not just worrying about running and marketing a business. Let's look at some of Winfrey's tips for making yourself better.

## SELF-LOVE AND SELF-BELIEF

Winfrey knows it's important to understand that self-worth, self-esteem, and self-love are vitally important assets. "The more you praise and celebrate your life, the more there is in life to celebrate," she says. You can prove that to yourself over and over every day by taking care of yourself. If you look after number one, then you are in a much better position to look after others.

Having a high opinion of yourself is good—this is not about being egotistical, it is about knowing your strengths. I'm a huge advocate of knowing your worth. You need to regard yourself and your thoughts and opinions as being valuable, valid, and important. There should be no need to apologise for wanting to improve your own life. Believing in yourself and having a strong sense of self-worth directly affects your actions on a daily basis, and those actions affect your results. So it all starts upstairs!

Everyone will eventually face a fork in the road. Too many of us choose the easy path. That way leads to giving up, to no longer putting in an effort or striving to succeed. The hard choice, the hard way, is to remain focused and to keep going, and this is doubly important because you become the decisions you make. If you commit to believing in yourself, to believing that you have merit, and that you are a worthy person who deserves to be loved and respected, then you are well on the way to success.

## LOOK FOR POSSIBILITIES

We all have limitations or disadvantages or handicaps of some sort or another. When we have a task to complete and one of our limitations stands in our way, we have to maintain our belief and desire to complete the task and, if possible, do so by finding another method. If you can't reach your goal by going along a certain pathway, find another pathway.

If you wait for success in life, you will be waiting a very long time. Don't sit around waiting and hoping and expecting things to happen. Make them happen. You need to become the instigator or the catalyst of your own good fortune—get out there and get what you want done. As Oprah says, "the biggest adventure you can take is to live the life of your dreams."

## WINFREY'S THOUGHTS ON RELATIONSHIPS

We are the people we are according to the people we are closest to. If a person is bad for your life, even if they are close or a member of your family, it is the right thing to move away from that person. If somebody has little or no respect for you, you should walk away quickly and as far as possible. "Lots of people want to ride with you in the limo, but what you want is someone who will take the bus with you when the limo breaks down," Winfrey says.

We are all capable of making a choice. We make a choice about the people we associate with, and are responsible for our own relationships.

## HAPPINESS AND BEING AT PEACE

Being able to forgive someone is a brilliant characteristic, but the forgiveness you offer is also a wonderful form of liberation for you. When you are able to understand the wrong you have done and can offer a fulsome and sincere apology, you are setting yourself free. Think about a time in your life when you just got over something by saying "it's ok" and accepting it.

You are in control of your happiness. You have the power within yourself to make your life peaceful and as happy as possible. You do not need external sources or resources. Remember, life is too short to be without happiness, forgiveness, love, laughter, and peace.

You control your own destiny and you decide whether you want to be a trusting person. You decide if tackling a task and helping others is worthwhile. While it is not just preferable but highly desirable that you learn from your mistakes, if you dwell on the past you never get a chance to envision a future.

You truly discover happiness and peace when you realise that every moment in life is precious and that spending time regretting decisions gives you no satisfaction and is a waste of energy. We need to live for the moment. You cannot live in the past and you cannot live in tomorrow. Make the most of the present.

One of Winfrey's great tips on improving your health and creating an attitude of peace is that by beginning each day with a brief session of meditation you can set yourself up for a relaxed, positive, and creative life. She says "the absolute key" to her success has been meditation, specifically at home under her oak trees, which she calls the 12 Apostles.

## HOW TO OVERCOME PREJUDICE

Most of us will face prejudice at some time or another in our lives though some suffer from it far more than others. Winfrey had a tough time at the beginning of her career and came up with the philosophy that the best way to respond to prejudice was to get better.

In the 1970s, when Winfrey became a newsreader on Nashville television, she was a rarity. She was a woman who didn't fit the stereotypical mould of a newsreader of those times, when newsreaders were predominantly white and male. When Oprah Winfrey landed her newsreading job she was subjected to significant prejudice but her response was simple: she set out to become the best in the business. "Excellence is the best deterrent to racism or sexism," she says.

## TAKING THE GOOD FROM THE BAD

Winfrey has a philosophy that says you should 'turn your wounds into wisdom'. She says, "Nothing happens to you, it always happens for you." She knows about this process from experience. In her early days in Baltimore, she suffered a calamity when a hairdresser damaged her hair so badly she was left with a bald head. Imagine how devastating that would be for someone who was on TV!

Many people would see this calamity as too difficult to overcome. Not only did Winfrey find a way to carry on working, by wearing a wig until her hair was repaired, but she also took advantage of the situation to improve her attitude and expertise in dealing with problems in life. She reframed this experience in her mind into something that could drive her forward, not hold her back.

She's faced trials regularly in her life. Her childhood was one of poverty growing up poor in Mississippi, an apartheid state. She was sexually abused as a child, and she became pregnant as a young teenager, but the baby boy (posthumously named Canaan) died in infancy. These were trying and even terrible times, but rather than despairing and giving up, Winfrey found a way to stay strong and move on. She believes that every single event in life happens for a reason and is an opportunity to choose love over fear.

Is there something in your past holding you back? Can you start seeing that experience as something you can become better because of ?

## DOING IT DIFFERENTLY

When we are children, our parents and our teachers tell us that there is a correct way of doing things. But in life, and certainly in business, we find a different set of rules.

For example, when Winfrey first became a television newsreader the tradition and convention was that the newsreader should speak in a dry, serious, and objective voice. She did not agree with this dictum. She believed that if a news item was sad and moving that she should express some emotion in the way she dealt with the subject.

Of course television producers were at first against this behaviour. But Winfrey was a great believer in being true to yourself, and people watching the news being read in this way warmed to this form of presentation. They loved her authenticity.

## YOU MAKE YOUR OWN LUCK

Becoming one of the richest women in the world obviously results from hard work and business acumen. Now, somebody who has created such wealth would have to have been lucky at some stage. Winfrey certainly doesn't argue with that. But she does not believe that luck simply falls out of the sky. "I feel luck is preparation meeting opportunity," she says.

She believes that if you wish to be a successful entrepreneur then you need to spend far less time hoping and far more time preparing. The point is that if you are seriously well prepared to be successful in business, if a lucky strike happens, you are in the prime position to take advantage.

## FINAL THOUGHT

Winfrey's success in television means that there is a vast online resource of her interviews and thinking. There are plenty of her publications available too. Outspoken and open, she shares her knowledge and experience with others. Through more than 35,000 interviews she's personally conducted with every type of person you could possibly imagine; her thought process is easy to study.

All this material emphasises the self, getting better, and improving who you are as a person. This can be overlooked in the business world, where the focus is often on attacking the competition through strategy. Like the story of Arianna Huffington later in this book, Winfrey's story is one of becoming a better person every day—an internal rather than external approach. A by-product of this internal process is the improvement of the lives of others, a wider view of success that brings others along for the ride.

# 5

## PIERRE OMIDYAR

Pierre Omidyar lives in Hawaii. Current net worth: US$8.1 billion.

### Pierre Omidyar, the digital auctioneer

Auctions have been around seemingly forever, with loud, fast-talking auctioneers at the centre of attention, bringing together buyers and sellers. But in 1995, at the very start of the public Internet, a 28-year-old named Pierre Omidyar brought the classic auction into the Digital Age with the now-famous eBay.

Omidyar had the idea to develop computer code that would enable people to do business with one another directly, selling collectible items by auction. A simple idea, the computer program would bring together buyers and sellers for a small fee, a commission on every sale completed. He wanted to call the site EchoBay, but the name was taken, leading to the short form eBay.

The auction website had phenomenal success almost from day one, quickly skyrocketing to approximately 800,000 online auctions per day. From commissions, Omidyar became wealthy very quickly. Today, eBay still ranks highly in web traffic lists, and Omidyar is worth billions.

Recently, Omidyar has become more interested in the media, launching an investigative news service reporting on business and civic affairs in the state of Hawaii, and in 2013, Omidyar joined forces with *The Huffington Post*. Omidyar was impressed by the work of Edward Snowden and the leaking of government information. As a result, Omidyar created another media outlet called First Look Media, and a number of prominent journalists have joined the organisation.

Omidyar was born in Paris, France, to Iranian parents, both of whom had been sent to France to study for their tertiary education. Omidyar's father became a surgeon and his mother a well-known academic. The family moved to the United States when Pierre was a young boy, his education taking place in American schools and universities. Omidyar didn't take an interest in computers until Year Nine in high school, but he went on to complete a bachelor's degree in computer science. "My parents made me believe I could do anything I wanted to do," he says. "They were really into empowering me."

Omidyar has a number of philosophies that may sound out of place in the ruthlessly competitive business world. Let's consider now what made him so successful.

## INSPIRATION AND KNOW-HOW

Two things made Omidyar's success happen:
- The idea or the inspiration
- The technical know-how or the ability to make it work.

Now, where you find inspiration and how you come up with brilliant ideas is perhaps the subject of a separate course of study. But assuming you do have a good, original idea, the question arises: do you have the technical know-how or the ability to translate that idea into a practical activity? Remember that Omidyar was a computer science student at both high school and university. He knew how to write code.

If you have some form of technical expertise, and if a brilliant idea pops into your head, then are you in a position to do something about transforming the idea into a reality? Have you got technical expertise in a particular field? Could you improve your level of knowledge? This is not to say you need to be an expert in everything, but you'll at least need to have people around you who are.

## DO SOMETHING AND TAKE ACTION

Sometimes we look for a secret ingredient that will make us successful. In the case of Omidyar, there was nothing secretive about what he did. He simply believed in himself, saw an opportunity and got on with it.

It is hard to believe now, but when Omidyar came up with the idea of what would become eBay, many people believed it would never work. Why would complete strangers want to get into a bidding war over a product that they couldn't touch and feel? How could you trust people that you've never met? Why would people bid for items that were located in another city, or another country, or another hemisphere? Good questions, but they didn't stop Omidyar from believing in his idea.

But believing was not enough. Many entrepreneurs have a great idea and believe in its potential, but they fall down because they fail to take action. Omidyar acted on his belief. The rest became history. Ideas are easy; execution is the key.

## HAVING A BACKUP PLAN

Entrepreneurship is risky, but an entrepreneur doesn't need to risk everything or start with nothing. Omidyar wasn't unemployed; he had a good job with a good income and came from a well-educated family. When he started working on the online auction idea, he didn't throw away his nine-to-five job.

Rather than ditch your present job and throw all of your time and money into your brilliant idea, why not copy Omidyar and build the concept, strategy and systems in your own time, then hit the tipping point when you can make the jump with lower risk?

## FOLLOW YOUR DREAM

The rule or principle of following your dream is vital for an entrepreneur. Can you think of one who didn't?

Omidyar had a dream as a computer science student and from an early age loved creating software programs. Wanting to be an entrepreneur just for the sake of being an entrepreneur or just to make money is not nearly as important as being an entrepreneur in an area or field or industry in which you have a passion.

Some years ago, Omidyar made the following statement:

> I always wanted to be involved with computers. I was just pursuing what I enjoy doing. I was pursuing my passion. It's not work really, if you're having fun. That was the case with me. You have to really believe in what you're doing, be passionate enough about it so that you'll put in the hours and hard work that it takes to actually succeed there, and then you'll be successful.

It's a fairly simple message. You shouldn't have to think much to discover your dream or your passion. It's something you've already been thinking about for years; you just need to give yourself permission to chase it! The secret is to channel your passion into your business. When you do that, working long and hard is no longer a chore because you love what you're doing. You don't have to motivate yourself because your dream is your motivation. Said differently, you shouldn't have to drag yourself out of bed to spend the day working when you find what you're passionate about.

## NICE GUYS DON'T ALWAYS FINISH LAST

Some people have the belief in the world of business that if you are too polite, too friendly, and too kind to your customers, you will suffer. The world is competitive and business is even more so. You are up against other people who are fighting for the same customers. They will stop at nothing to do the deal. They will do anything it takes to be successful. If you don't join them and think like them, or act like them, you will be defeated. It's a common philosophy.

However, Omidyar doesn't think like that. When he is looking to engage a new employee, he is not so much interested in their expertise and experience but rather asks himself the question, "Is this person nice?"

The whole point here is that he wants to work with people he will enjoy working with. It is the exact opposite of the statement that 'nice guys finish last'. Omidyar is a strong believer that nice guys finish first.

He has found that, by choosing to surround himself with people he trusts and likes and enjoys working with, there are two distinct benefits:

- Everyone is more productive
- Everyone enjoys coming to work.

Now if you had to choose two qualities or two characteristics that you would most like to have in your business, I would suggest that being more productive and looking forward to being at work would be right at the top of the list.

## THE IMPORTANCE OF VALUES

It's not good enough to simply think that you have a good principle or a good idea; you also need to do something practical about it. In the case of Omidyar and eBay, he drew up a document with a heading of Core Values. The two major points on this list were honesty and trust. Having drawn up a list of core values, he explained them to all employees and discussed how they could be put into practice.

Let's talk about the issue of honesty. Surveys show that for every one million transactions that take place on eBay, only 30 transactions result in somebody making a complaint about fraud or dishonesty. If you ran a business and a miniscule number of your customers were unhappy, would you be unhappy? Hardly. That's a phenomenally good rate of customer satisfaction.

Omidyar described his philosophy as follows:

> I founded the company on the notion that people were basically good and that if you give them the benefit of the doubt, you're rarely disappointed. Nice guys, a responsible company that has its heart in the right place—that's run by real human beings—it has to be successful, because if we weren't that way, eBay wouldn't be successful. It wouldn't be possible.

## EMPOWERING OTHERS, PROVIDING OPPORTUNITIES

Another key principle for Omidyar was to empower people to do business, to provide a space for people to create their own success. His site didn't sell his products to customers—he was just facilitating others to create their own business. He puts it this way: "I try to help people take ownership. Everything I've done is rooted in the notion that every human being is born equally capable. What people lack is equal opportunity." Before Facebook, before Twitter, before LinkedIn and other community sites, Omidyar was connecting people through commerce.

> What I'm really focused on is connecting people around shared interests, so together they can make good stuff happen. I'm more focused on helping people discover their power as individuals, but through those connections with one another.

## FINAL THOUGHT

In a nutshell, there are three lessons we can take from Omidyar:

- Don't just think about it, do it
- Live your dream
- Nice guys can finish first.

The beauty of the lessons from Omidyar are that they are so simple and so few. It's not good enough having an idea; you need to actually act on that idea. And if people, even people you highly regard, are critical and advise you that your plan or idea is a non-starter, you must have the courage to persevere if you believe in it.

If you are going to get involved in a project, it's far better if you are passionate about that project. In the case of Omidyar, his passion was for computer science. He was passionate about creating a program that would work and he had the skills and expertise to create such a program; the perfect combination.

He strongly believes that you need to draw up a list of core values, with two prominent points being honesty and trust, and that you need to carry out those core values in everything you do. Yes, you can be successful and nice at the same time. When I do this for my companies I only have three values at most for each company, and those three must mean something that reflects the brand. They must be something that each team member can remember and embrace in their core, and importantly these values must be reflected in the way we do business inside and out.

# 6

## LARRY PAGE

Larry Page lives in California. Current net worth US$40.9 billion.

### Take a page out of Larry's entrepreneurship playbook

This famous entrepreneur made his fortune by introducing a new word to the English language. This word has become so integrated into our vocabulary that we actually use it as a verb: to Google something. 'Google' it.

Born in 1973 in America, Larry Page created a revolutionary search engine—and a company called Google Inc.—that now helps billions of people every day. "Basically, our goal is to organise the world's information and to make it universally accessible and useful," says Page. That's a big goal, but one that Google is on the way to achieving.

In its short life, Google has grown rapidly, has a work force of more than 60,000 people with offices in many countries, and is involved in a wide range of applications, programs, and projects.

At the turn of the 21st century, there was no shortage of enthusiastic investors for Google. A few short years later those investors—and Larry Page—would be, as they say, rolling in it. However, money wasn't the motivation for Page. "If we were motivated by money, we would have sold the company a long time ago and ended up on a beach," he says.

The significance of the Google invention is mind-boggling. Imagine the Net without a search engine. Before Google, the Web had about 10 million documents or sites with many more links. Trying to build a web crawler that could make contact with any or all of the links was a daunting task. Page realised that if he could come up with a method to count and relate the various links on the Web then it would become a much more valuable place.

At university, Page was joined by fellow student Sergey Brin, who was equally fascinated by the project. Page's dormitory room was soon overflowing with computers and other equipment. The very early search engine they put together was housed on the Stanford University website. People could suddenly find information and pages on the Internet rapidly. It was both mind-blowing and ground-breaking for its time.

## AN EARLY START

Page's interest in computers and programming comes from his genes and upbringing. His father and his mother were both computer experts, and taught and lectured at university. His father was a pioneer in computer science and artificial intelligence when the subjects were in their early days in the 1960s. Larry Page was the first student in his primary school to submit an assignment using a word processor.

Page remembers a childhood with all sorts of computers and computer magazines lying around the house. He and his older brother would take things apart simply to find out how they worked. Page went on to study computer science at university. After his bachelor's degree in Michigan, Page began a PhD thesis at Stanford University on the topic of exploring the mathematical properties of the World Wide Web.

Now let's examine some of the principles that made Page and Google so successful.

## LOOK FOR A PARTNER AS A PARTNER

The enormous success of Google Inc. can be traced to a number of factors. One factor is the partnership between Page and Brin. They work so well together. Yes, they both have analytical minds and are both aware of IT and associated fields of endeavour. They complement one another but are not identical. You need to be free to express your opinion and ideas while knowing that the other person will treat you

...ct and appreciate your contribution. It is the ...sonal qualities too, which count. You need the same set of rules, values, and attitudes. You need independent thinkers but with everyone pulling in the same direction.

## MANAGING PEOPLE WELL

One of the first things you will notice when you study the working habits of Larry Page is that he doesn't like traditional management structures. He's long been an advocate of not having middle-level management. "We don't have as many managers as we should, but we would rather have too few than too many," he says. His ideal work colleague is someone who is really good at what they do and does it naturally without having to be told.

Looking at the type of company he has created—with the world's top talent applying to work for him in droves, and staff happiness, longevity and productivity at one of the highest levels of all modern companies—whatever he and Brin are doing as managers is clearly working.

Page is also super-intelligent when it comes to reading people. After more than 10 years with Google, half of his top product managers were still employed in the company. They are extremely wealthy and have no need to work ever again, but they are still working for Google because they love the company and what it does. Page had a big hand in selecting those people.

 My job as a leader is to make sure

everybody in the company has great opportunities, and that they feel they're having a meaningful impact and are contributing to the good of society.

Page advocates the following specific principles in running a business:

- Don't delegate but do as much as you can yourself, which means that things happen faster.
- Don't interrupt people who are working successfully. Don't get in their way.
- Never become a bureaucrat.
- The key to success in the company is an idea. Ideas have no respect for age or experience. Examine the idea not the person who suggested it.
- The word 'no' can be the worst thing to say to anyone. If you do say 'no', then you have to help the person find a way to make the task work.

GO BIG...

If you need to make changes to your operation, Page reckons that small changes rarely work. "Especially in technology, we need revolutionary change, not incremental change," Page says. That's not to say that everything he tries revolutionises the world, but he believes that you should accept an audacious idea and let it run. If it means turning things upside down to achieve success, then do it.

A perfect example of this is when Google started to tackle the huge field of artificial intelligence. All of their work came to naught, or did it? As a result of that activity, they came up with their famous advertisement targeting system that produces half of the massive income that Google receives. The big idea didn't work as originally planned, but because it was big it created something else, which was a massive hit.

## ...BUT REMEMBER THE SMALL

Incremental change shouldn't be discounted, however. The product should never be seen as complete or finished. It can always be polished or improved or made more flexible. Once the program is up and running, tinkering and adding new bits and pieces—always with the aim to improve—is what will keep that application or product popular. This is another reason why customers love Google; there is always something new happening. As customers, we want to know that things have been improved or have new capabilities. That sort of attitude from Google keeps us hanging around.

## NEVER GIVE UP

You've heard that piece of advice from every guru and entrepreneur and at every seminar and networking session you have attended—even mine. But it is so true. Page had this brilliant idea that books should be converted to digital format. He was thinking about that type of project in the mid-1990s. He never gave up, and it was almost ten years before the first book was made digital.

What about the Street View on Google Maps? That idea took many years to come to fruition. Many millions of people looking for a location can now not only find it on a map, but they can also view a photo of the location. They can stand at the front of the location and get a 360° view of everything in that street. It's a brilliant concept but one that needed time and encouragement. 'Never give up' has built Google (and now it's umbrella company, Alphabet) and is a key to Page's success.

## INNOVATION IN OPERATION

Obviously, Google and Larry Page have made the development of new products and ideas into an art form. But what does this mean for you in your role as an entrepreneur? Well, Page distinguishes between the creative side of Google and the business operation of the juggernaut. These two arms are both essential yet both are separate.

You need to come up with new technology and better ways of operating the technology you already have. That is a given. That is an ongoing process. But you also need to operate the business in such a way that the creative arm is given its head. You need to be sleek and solid, do away with red tape and not get in the way of the creative people. In fact, it's just the opposite. The business strategies and business operations need to complement the creative side of your business. Get both of these factors right and the combined power gives you enormous potential: a key strategy Page has run with.

## FINAL THOUGHT

Larry Page, most would agree, has made the world a better place. When you draw up your list of goals featuring your projected growth, profit forecasts and the like, will you include anything about being a better corporate citizen or about trying to leave a positive and helpful mark on the world?

We're not talking about creating a massive charitable foundation and donating vast sums of money to worthy causes—although that would be nice. No, just in the everyday business of being an entrepreneur you could always try to consider your team, suppliers and customers. You could build better and more lasting relationships. You could be a successful businessperson and still be a nice human being. With the massive business Google has become, it's easy to see that Larry Page is determined to be successful but also to be a decent and helpful person in both small and large ways.

Of course Page is brilliant. But he is also smart. He knows that recruiting the best people can only improve Google and Alphabet, and help it continue to grow and to be even more profitable and successful. The message is simple: surround yourself with the right people and treat everyone with respect.

Page had an ideal childhood, having parents who

were skilled and interested in digital technology. But Page had to go beyond his upbringing. He tackled different degrees and worked hard. The key is to take what knowledge and talents you have and turn them to your advantage in being a successful entrepreneur.

# 7

## JEFF BEZOS

Jeff Bezos lives in Washington, USA. Current net worth: US$73.3 billion.

### Delivering success the Jeff Bezos way

Only five years ago, most people visited bricks-and-mortar shops to buy a book. Now, bookstores are going out of business as online book sales dominate. You may have never heard of the American entrepreneur Jeff Bezos, but you have heard of the online book marketplace he founded: Amazon.com. The value of shares in Amazon have enjoyed a meteoric rise, and it is believed that the value of his shareholdings equates to around US$30 billion.

Today, millions of people buy eBooks—or electronic books—online, a business popularised and perfected by Amazon, a gigantic business operation. And Amazon sells a lot more than just books. The site has branched out into the sale of electronics, car tyres, and even kids' toys. It's a virtual marketplace like no other. And there's more: Amazon's proprietary eBook reading device, the Kindle, is universally recognised and regularly used by millions. The business of publishing and selling books has been revolutionised largely due to Amazon.

Its founder, Jeff Bezos, certainly had a humble beginning. His teenage mother and father had a short marriage, and Jeff was relocated frequently. As a child, he had an interest in building things, solving puzzles, and finding out how things worked. He was an outstanding student at college, where he studied computer science.

After college, he worked in a variety of well-paid jobs, some on Wall Street, before deciding that online trading was the boom niche. At this time, several state governments in the United States declared there would be no sales tax on the sale of electronic books. Knowing this, Bezos drew up his plan for what would become Amazon. And the rest, as they say, is history.

Bezos can be compared favourably with another entrepreneur, Sir Richard Branson. Both men are interested in space flight, with Bezos creating a company that aims to build hotels and colonies in space for millions of people to live in as they orbit the globe. If nothing else, Bezos is a forward thinker.

His donations to charity are well known and his business interests are many and varied. In 2013, he purchased the prestigious newspaper *The Washington Post*. The fee was reported to be US$250 million, paid in cash. If ever there were an entrepreneur to study, Jeff Bezos is the perfect example.

## FORWARD THINKING

You can analyse the activities of entrepreneurs in many ways: their vision, their ambition, their preparation and their dedication. But one important aspect you should always consider is their forward thinking. Sometimes you can get too busy working on the day-to-day aspects of your business and end up giving little or no attention to the future.

> We believe that a fundamental measure of our success will be the shareholder value we create over the *long term*... Because of our emphasis on the *long term*, we may make decisions and weigh trade-offs differently than some companies.

Where do you sit when it comes to forward thinking? As an entrepreneur, are you fixated on the present? Do you have a long-term plan or vision like Bezos does?

Because you are concentrating so much on the present, simply getting through the day, fighting a fire or trying to just make a sale, you can at times lose sight of what is happening in a month or six months or a year down the track. The decisions you make today could well be based simply on what you're doing today. Yet by adopting the Bezos philosophy of forward thinking, you change the way you act today.

## EXTEND YOUR HORIZONS

As an entrepreneur, you know that you are in a highly competitive business. By creating a business plan or marketing plan, or with just some basic goal setting, you give yourself clarity and the best possible chance of not just surviving but thriving.

But don't forget there are dozens, perhaps hundreds of other entrepreneurs working in a similar or related field to you. Many of them are chasing the same customers. So how can you give yourself an advantage?

Bezos believes that if you think further than the length of the standard business plan, you push yourself into both a mental and physical situation where you have to do certain things to achieve your goals. This is how Bezos sums it up: "If everything you do needs to work on a three-year time horizon, then you're competing against a lot of people. But if you're willing to invest on a seven-year time horizon, you're now competing against a fraction of those people, because very few companies are willing to do that. Just by lengthening the time horizon, you can engage in endeavours that you could never otherwise pursue."

## SO HOW DOES HE DO IT?

Many entrepreneurs will say that they agree wholeheartedly with this philosophy of thinking long-term. But when it comes to doing something practical about it, they come up with all sorts of excuses:

- I'm far too busy at the moment
- I don't have staff to tackle certain things, so I'm tied up at work
- Nobody knows where future trends will go, so I'll be wasting my time.

Bezos takes a hands-on approach. Sure, he talks the talk but he also walks the walk. He goes out of his way to make time to think about the future. Perhaps it's a case of less haste, more speed. Perhaps if you set aside time to do nothing but think about the future and plan for it, you might not only develop an excellent business plan for the long-term, but might start making better strategic decisions on a day-to-day basis. Thinking long-term helps you short-term too.

If you want to follow Bezos and do something practical about forward thinking, you need to ask yourself the following questions:

- How good am I at forward thinking?
- Do my forward-thinking skills need a facelift?
- What practical steps can I take to get better at forward thinking?

## THE PAST IS THE FUTURE

As an entrepreneur, you are obviously thinking about what you can do to be successful in the future. One thing that many entrepreneurs do is to try to predict trends or inventions or discoveries.

For example, if in the 1970s you were able to

predict the information superhighway, the Internet, and perhaps even social media, then you would be both a genius and presumably incredibly wealthy. So naturally, many an entrepreneur will scratch his or her head and think, 'What is the next big thing? How can I be a part of that?'

Jeff Bezos understands that way of thinking, but he adopts a different approach, which puts him in an even stronger position. You could ask two questions to sum up the way Jeff Bezos thinks:

- What is likely to be invented in the next five to 10 years?
- What is likely to still be popular in the next five to 10 years?

There's a not-so-subtle difference here. If you ask the second question and get the right answer, then you're giving yourself an excellent chance of becoming a successful entrepreneur based on how Bezos thinks. In the case of Bezos, he asked the second question and got two answers:

- People want to be able to purchase goods in the simplest way and at the cheapest price
- People want speedy delivery.

In the above situation, you are definitely thinking about the future, you are definitely doing forward planning, but you are doing it based on the current situation. You're looking at what is working today and asking the question, what would still be working in five or ten years' time? Now, nobody can be absolutely certain, but because of the success of low prices and speedy delivery, it's hard to believe that masses of customers will not be happy with this situation. We all want low prices and speedy delivery. As Bezos says, "You can build a business strategy around the things that are stable in time."

Based on that philosophy, look at your business and see which parts of it are working well and why, and then create a business plan and policies to maintain your success well into the future.

## WILL YOU HAVE ANY REGRETS?

Like many entrepreneurs, Bezos started out working a nine-to-five job, with a boss, job security, a superannuation plan and an idea of his own.

His victory here came when he asked himself the question, "Do I want to live with regret?" He fast-forwarded his life about 50 years. He imagined himself as an old man and he asked himself these questions:

- If I don't take the risk and become an entrepreneur, will I regret never having started the new career?
- If I do take the risk and fail, will I regret my decision?

His biggest regret would be to fail. But which situation would cause the greater regret? Would it be not having taken the risk at all? Or would it be taking the risk and not being successful?

He believes the greater regret would be the first answer: not taking the risk at all. The question he asked was this: "When I'm 80 years old, what will I regret the most?"

He used the answer to help drive him to leave his secure Wall Street employment and branch out on his own as an entrepreneur and founder of Amazon.

So ask yourself, which would be your greater regret?

## DO YOU HAVE DEEP POCKETS?

Many an entrepreneur hesitates before going into business, or, once in business, hesitates to expand. The reason for this hesitation is that they have little or no capital. Do you have deep pockets? If the answer is no, then what should you do? Not start the business? Hold off on any expansion plans?

Some entrepreneurs see a lack of funds as being a serious impediment to their growth. Bezos takes a different approach. In fact, he sees the lack of resources as a benefit. That's right, as a benefit! His thinking is as follows: "I think frugality drives innovation, just like other constraints do. One of the only ways to get out of a tight box is to invent your way out."

He is right. If you had stacks of money, your approach to starting or expanding your business would be different than the approach of somebody who has little or no money.

Having now met tens of thousands of entrepreneurs globally, this would have to be one of, if not the top reason that many hesitate to 'just get started'.

This does not mean you should put yourself into debt, but rather, you should look upon a limited budget as an incentive to find new ways operate in a leaner fashion, not as a massive obstacle to progress. The reality is that almost all business success stories started with little or no capital—so what's your excuse now?

## ONLY ORDER TWO PIZZAS

As an entrepreneur, one of the key factors of your business is productivity. The more productive you are, the greater your chances of success. So what can you do to improve productivity?

The Jeff Bezos philosophy is to order two pizzas instead of six, eight, or ten. If you are having a meeting and you order a large amount of food, a considerable amount of time will be wasted by having so many choices. More time will be spent looking for a napkin or a plate, or getting another piece of pizza, and less time will be spent being productive in that meeting.

How does this relate to your situation? Think about your business meetings. Are there unnecessary distractions? Is your desire to develop a team spirit and camaraderie in your business interrupting the actual flow of business? Bezos has some pretty clear ideas on the subject:

 The fewer people involved in a project, the less distraction, the more productivity. Teams that are excessively large are bound to be less effective, because in order for things to get done in those settings, more voices will have to be heard. And they're not necessarily the ones worth hearing.

## FINAL THOUGHT

Jeff Bezos is a risk taker with a great deal of knowledge about computer science and how the Internet works. He has always been a forward thinker with a different take. Rather than concentrate on what might happen in five or ten years' time as far as new inventions are concerned, he chooses to concentrate on what might still be happening in five or ten years' time, and concentrated on providing those goods and services.

His success has not dimmed his interest in other things, or his willingness to contribute financially to causes he believes are deserving. The things we can extract from that statement should ring true with every entrepreneur:

- Think long-term strategy
- Get ahead—what is going to be the demand in your industry in the next five years?
- Helping others who are less fortunate benefits everyone.

While some may never reach the global success levels and financial rewards of entrepreneurs such as Jeff Bezos, we can learn from his approach to business, the way he goes about his business, and his many pieces of advice. When that advice comes from the creator of a business with a share price around US$300 per share, every entrepreneur should listen.

Finally, Bezos is great at asking himself good questions. Questions to challenge himself and improve constantly.

Are you asking yourself the right questions?

# 8

# BILL GATES

Bill Gates lives in Medina, Washington, USA. Current net worth: US$85.7 billion.

Ruling the computer business, one window at a time

Author Alexandra Robbins predicts that someday the "geeks shall inherit the Earth". Looking at our next entrepreneur, it seems that the geeks already have. Bill Gates, the founder of Microsoft, admitted once "I'm a geek." He even said, "If your culture doesn't like geeks, you are in real trouble. Be nice to nerds. Chances are you'll end up working for one."

Gates went from teenage computer geek to one of the most famous entrepreneurs by contributing fundamental products to increase the productivity and popularity of personal computers. "It's pretty amazing to go from a world where computers were unheard of and very complex to where they're a tool of everyday life," Gates says. "That was the dream that I wanted to make come true, and in a large part it's unfolded as I'd expected." His coding and business acumen made Microsoft a household name. He's since turned into an investor in global social initiatives. His entrepreneurship clearly deserves a close look.

Gates was born on October 28, 1955, into a well-off family. His father, William H. Gates, was a lawyer, his lifestyle was upper middle-class, and in the early 1970s he attended high school at the private Lakeside School. Lakeside School had one of the first personal computers, and Gates programmed it with the simple language BASIC, creating a tic-tac-toe game.

A computer company named Computer Center Corporation allowed Gates and his friends—including future business partner Paul Allen—to use its system. However, they were banned for a number of months after exploiting bugs in the system that allowed them to access more time online. Gates went on to program a piece of software that did payroll for a company called Information Sciences, and, at age 17, he programmed traffic counters with Allen. Gates did have a mischievous side—at one point he created a program for his high school that made class schedules for students. However, he inserted a line of code that assigned more girls to his own classes.

At the end of high school, Gates scored extremely high on standardised tests. He tells the story:

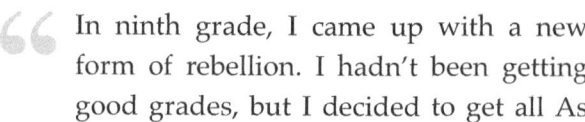 In ninth grade, I came up with a new form of rebellion. I hadn't been getting good grades, but I decided to get all As

without taking a book home. I didn't go to math class, because I knew enough and had read ahead, and I placed within the top 10 people in the nation on an aptitude exam.

Gates easily got into Harvard University, where he met Steve Ballmer, a future Microsoft CEO. Gates wrote successful programs as part of class assignments, but he was more interested in starting a business. He dropped out of Harvard after his first year, and he started a software company with Allen called Micro-Soft—the name was changed to Microsoft in 1976.

Let's now look at some of the principles that turned Gates into a computer-industry maven and leading citizen of the world.

## SIMPLE BUT FUNDAMENTAL IDEAS

Gates's business success is rooted in a simple idea. In the late-1970s, personal computers were bursting on the scene. The hardware was getting smaller and more powerful, but computers couldn't run on hardware alone. Manufacturers needed software to run the machines. A deft programmer, Gates came up with a simple interpreter code. His early code was stolen and redistributed by other computer enthusiasts—a common problem in the software business—causing Gates to write an open letter to ask that people pay for his software.

Around 1980, the major hardware manufacturer

IBM was introducing a personal computer to the market and Gates offered disk-operating software (DOS) to the company. Gates was smart, rather than selling the software copyright and losing control, he licensed the DOS code because he predicted that IBM's hardware would be copied and replicated by others.

He was right. Other manufacturers cloned the IBM system, creating their own personal computers as the market exploded; perhaps his initial experience with his code being stolen prompted him to use the licensing model. This meant his company was paid upfront, during the installation stage, and the cost was passed on to consumers and businesses. Software piracy still existed, but it didn't dampen revenue nearly as much.

> The way to be successful in the software world is to come up with breakthrough software, and so whether it's Microsoft Office or Windows, it's pushing that forward. New ideas, surprising the marketplace, so good engineering and good business are one in the same.

Can you think of a way in your business to develop similar products that are unique and allow upfront payment?

## CONSTANT CHANGE

In business, you don't want to get stuck on one iteration of your product either—it risks obsolescence.

"Most of our competitors," Gates says, "were one-product wonders... They would do their one product, but never get their engineering sorted out."

Entrepreneurs need to be always thinking about how to make their products better, or invent into new ones. Gates identified a problem with his operating system in the early 1980s. DOS computers required users to have a level of competence in coding commands—commands directed to the computer, such as how to run a program, were performed only by typing them in. This meant that many early personal computers were not user-friendly, and they were more often only used by computer-savvy enthusiasts.

> Software innovation, like almost every other kind of innovation, requires the ability to collaborate and share ideas with other people, and to sit down and talk with customers and get their feedback and understand their needs.

With this problem in mind, Gates and his team at Microsoft started to develop a solution: they would create a graphical, desktop-style operating system with small, adjustable windows that users could click and resize with the touch of a new technology called a 'mouse'.

On November 20, 1985, Microsoft introduced the first retail version of the Windows graphical operating software. PC users will remember the many versions of the software: Windows 95, Windows 98, Windows

2000, Windows XP, and so on. Associated programs like Microsoft Word and Excel became the de facto standard in all businesses, even weathering a shift to open-source software recently.

There seems to be no end to the software that made Gates the richest man in the world. Do you have ideas for products that can be continually updated and refined? One-off products can become obsolete, but products that can be updated bring in a long-term revenue stream or recurring payments.

FAILING AT PERFECTION

The computer business is a particularly difficult arena for the perfectionist. Bugs are the norm in software. Hardware-manufacturing processes sometimes don't live up to a high standard in a throwaway society where the solution to a product problem is to buy a new one. It's a business where failure is almost expected. Even Gates says, "I'm never fully satisfied with any Microsoft product."

Yet Gates wouldn't have it any other way. He argues, "Success is a lousy teacher. It seduces smart people into thinking they can't lose." Problems with your products should drive you to improve them and satisfy customers. Gates loves to get product feedback from his customers. "That's how we improve," he says. In some companies, particularly unhappy customers are pushed away and forgotten, considered simply a nuisance. But Gates advised that "Your most unhappy customers are your greatest source of learning."

He argues that it's important to measure everything you do, such as performance and customer satisfaction, not just revenues. "It's fine to celebrate success," he says, "but it is more important to heed the lessons of failure."

Gates is also famous for spending a huge part of his working days with Microsoft clients getting feedback on their products directly, and not just through surveys once a year.

### A STRONG TASKMASTER

A highly competitive man, Bill Gates was not known to coddle his employees. While softer today, and having a democratic leadership style (which means he loves feedback and multiple thoughts on ideas and direction), he was a tough leader in the 1980s and 1990s, and he was somewhat distant with people.

He pushed employees hard to create a variety of platforms to extend Microsoft's tentacles into just about every aspect of the computer business. If he saw any errors or mistakes in an employee's work, he could be a blunt critic. One story goes that an employee was making a presentation when Gates stopped him and said, "That's the stupidest thing I've ever heard." The employee then had to scramble to satisfy Gates.

 One thing I've always loved about the culture at Microsoft is there is nobody who is tougher on us, in terms of what we need to learn and do better, than the people in the company itself. You can walk down these halls, and they'll tell you, 'We need to do usability better, push this or that frontier'.

How tough are you on your employees? Do you believe in being blunt or do you prefer a diplomatic style? Sometimes entrepreneurs with high standards prefer the blunt approach as it gets to the heart of the matter quickly—and certainly Gates didn't have to worry about whether people liked him. All that mattered was doing the best work.

## OVERCOMING SETBACKS

Microsoft became so successful with its licensing practices that by 1999, Windows operating systems had achieved almost 95% market share, a great achievement for any business in any industry. At the time, the only competition was Apple, but it was only a minor player in personal computers despite its Windows-like desktop system.

Microsoft's great success proved, however, to raise questions. It was so successful, its software so widespread; that the US Government alleged it used antitrust practices. Lawyers for the US Government said that the company was essentially a monopoly and had used unfair business practices to stop other competitors from accessing the market. In a grand occasion, Gates actually had to testify in court, and his responses were famous—now collected for posterity in YouTube videos—for not getting to the point.

A judge agreed with the prosecution, and the initial remedy was to break up the company into smaller parts. Eventually, Microsoft settled the case and was only required to share some elements of its software with other companies. Gates survived the onslaught and Microsoft has continued to thrive, moving into new areas such as cloud computing and tablet computers.

## GIVING BACK TO THE COMMUNITY

If an entrepreneur reaches the pinnacle of success, what's next? Gates recognised that being a successful entrepreneur was not enough. His wealth has made it easy for him to go beyond just selling software and to influence the world in other ways.

In 2000, he stepped down as the CEO of Microsoft, although he continues to advise the company. Since then, he's chosen to spend more and more time on his charitable organisation, the Bill & Melinda Gates Foundation, the largest private charitable foundation in the world.

The great entrepreneurs in American history—think Andrew Carnegie and John D. Rockefeller—understood that they had to use their wealth to buy more than just a new airplane or a new mansion or a million-dollar car.

I'm certainly well taken care of in terms of food and clothes. Money has no utility to me beyond a certain point. Its utility is entirely in building an organisation and getting the resources out to the poorest in the world.

The Bill & Melina Gates Foundation was designed to take the billions Gates wasn't spending and use it to fund global initiatives related to development and health. They focus on the problems that governments and private businesses ignore. "Capitalism is this wonderful thing that motivates people," Gates says. "It causes wonderful inventions to be done. But in this area of diseases of the world at large, it's really let us down." Through his foundation, he can take risks that perhaps capitalists and governments cannot afford to take. Today the foundation has a US$42.3 billion endowment, with 1223 employees. Gates even convinced his billionaire friend Warren Buffett to donate significantly to the organisation.

The poor are usually ignored by businesses because they have no money to spend. However, Gates argues that, "We make the future sustainable when we invest in the poor, not when we insist on their suffering." He applies his business knowledge to bring together global stakeholders, and in his words, "establish a set of measurable, actionable and consensus-built goals focused on extreme poverty".

Some important projects have included funding for micro-finance projects in impoverished nations, nano-membrane toilets for countries with sanitation problems, and even a microbial fuel cell that converts urine to electricity. Can you think of ways to turn your entrepreneurship into something more for the world at large?

## FINAL THOUGHT

Bill Gates was the classic computer geek, working for hours alone in a room with a computer and his unique intellect. Writer Malcolm Gladwell also argues that Gates grew up at an important time, a time when personal computers were in their infancy. He combined brains with some luck to be involved at the initial stage of a revolution in human communication.

Gates employed tough and disciplined business leadership with great vision for the future to dominate the world's computer market, while giving people the tools to communicate better and work more efficiently. His career wasn't without its failures and challenges, but he overcame them.

While many people wish to be rich and would celebrate being the world's richest person, Gates says, "I wish I wasn't… There's nothing good that comes out of that. You get more visibility as a result of it." On the positive side, Gates has been able to use his riches to make a great difference in the world, not just for the people buying his products but also for the people who need his help the most—the world's poor.

Sometimes people talk about giving as an afterthought to business success, but I believe it can go hand in hand if you find or start a cause that you care about and proportion some of your revenues to that cause. Linking success to giving is a powerful and fulfilling concept.

# 9

## AMANCIO ORTEGA

Amancio Ortega lives in Spain. Current net worth: US$70.2 billion.

The reclusive Spanish billionaire.

The man who created the clothing empire Inditex, including the Zara chain, wears basic clothes to work —none of which are manufactured by his company— and eats lunch in the staff cafeteria with his fellow workers.

This is the world's fourth richest man, according to *Forbes*, the reclusive Spanish billionaire Amancio Ortega Gaona. Ortega lives in a comfortable but not ostentatious apartment in Galicia, Spain. He rarely gives interviews, and when he decided to open up his company to public shareholders the meeting was front-page news. He was born in 1936, but it wasn't until the end of the 20th century that a photo of this mystery man was first published.

From a poor family, Ortega left school early. His father worked on the railways and his mother was employed as a maid. Ortega's first job was working in a small business, making shirts.

Ortega's first manufactured item of clothing was a quilted bathrobe. Since then, his empire has expanded greatly with a variety of labels and thousands of retail outlets. In 2011, he announced he would retire from Inditex. Despite his retirement, he continues to be influential in the business community.

Speaking in the style of the Spanish romantic, Ortega says the goal of his business is to "attempt to seduce the customer with the latest fashion, the finest design, and the most attentive service".

Now let's look at some principles of Ortega's success.

## STEPPING STONES

As an entrepreneur, you may be thinking that you want to launch your company by tackling one big idea right from the start. That might work, and it is something I've done in early ventures; however, the method used by Ortega was just the opposite. He started small. Very small.

When he was in his mid-20s, he became the manager of a local clothing shop. Here he noticed that a number of wealthy customers were only interested in expensive clothing. The store became a niche market and grew slowly. He didn't throw a vast amount of money into his early activity.

He diversified into the rag trade, buying cheap

material from one part of Spain and selling it to a variety of shops all over the other parts of the country. Then he started making clothes, but again in a low-key way. He was very specific in concentrating on bathrobes at the beginning—an almost singular item of business.

When he created the fashion brand Zara in 1975, he had already spent half his life working in the clothing industry. Before he began his clothing chain, Ortega already knew a great deal about manufacturing garments, about different types of customers, about suppliers, and about retailing. He didn't expand overnight. Ortega opened his first fashion boutique in 1975 and it took him 12 years before he reached his 100th store. He learned all he needed working for others first, and built his knowledge using OPM (other people's money).

Beginning can sometimes be a problem for today's entrepreneurs, but expanding can be a killer. You need to be sure that when you expand, the growth is not so quick that it damages your entire operation, and having a deep knowledge of a market allows you to anticipate both problems and opportunities on the path.

## VISION IS ALWAYS IMPORTANT

Yes, Ortega started one clothing shop with a single brand, but he had a vision. He was able to see the potential of having more outlets and more brands. As a result, apart from the Zara brand, he created Kiddy's

Class, Oysho, Pull, Zara Home and Stradivarius, among others.

The brands are not only known in Spain, so his vision and hard work meant that his success was repeated around the world. One recent survey found he had some 14,000 members of staff working in 7,500 stores in 73 countries. If you have a good idea and a great product, there can be a whole global market waiting to do business with you. This is the best time in history for an *almost* instant global brand capacity if you do it right and have vision and a good mentor!

## SPREAD YOUR ASSETS AROUND

Many entrepreneurs are fixated on the success of their business and that is easy to understand. But there will come a time, sometimes sooner rather than later, when you'll experience a dip in your business. Trade will not always be as bullish as before. This could have nothing to do with you and could be an overall malaise caused by an economic downturn or a government change.

If you have all your money tied up in your business and things go pear-shaped, you may not be in a position to get the business going again once the good times come around. Ortega knew this and invested.

Many people would invest profits back into the business—generally a good idea—but Ortega made sure that he invested significant amounts of his wealth in other areas such as property, tourism, gas, and real estate. In other words, he makes money from more than one specific part of the economy. Personally, I focus on businesses funding more business ventures, real-estate holdings and stocks for long term, therefore spreading the risks. But the key here is to invest well and diversify.

## HOW TO BE A GREAT CEO

As you know, the CEO is vital to the success of your business. Whether you're ready now for this person (financially or emotionally!) it's a natural progression for a true entrepreneur. Why? Because a true entrepreneur will have many ventures ahead of them and will need to have people in charge of key businesses so that they can step away and create the next one in their empire.

So how do you find and select such a person? Do you hire from within? Do you use a head-hunter to catch the right person for your needs?

Perhaps Ortega can help us take a different perspective on the issue. He had little or no education and thus no formal qualifications. He went, as is often said, to the 'School of Hard Knocks'. As an entrepreneur, we need to take a total or broad approach to the hiring of managers and a CEO in particular.

Does the right person have to come with the so-called appropriate qualifications? If yes, then Ortega would miss the cut. And yet he served as CEO of a massive empire for many years, and the business thrived. Beware of prejudice and don't be afraid to look outside the normal list of applicants. Hiring the right person is paramount, so take your time!

## AGAINST THE TREND

When you look at fashion houses around the world in the last 50 years, none of them operated the way Ortega's did. He did not see himself as a traditional retailer of clothes. The entrepreneur set out to build his clothing empire on two basic principles:

- Give the customers what they want
- Get it to them faster than anyone else can.

Now many of you may say that these are not unique principles. Many businesses, perhaps even most businesses, aim to give the customers what they want. In this particular case we're talking about fashion. This is a fickle business with many failed ventures in its wake. Who knows what is going to be in demand next season or the season after that? Ortega saw the approach of getting what a customer wants on shelves quicker than anyone else as key, as well as changing stock often, unlike many rivals with much fewer ranges and longer shelf lives. He wanted customers to come back weekly, not quarterly and it's this approach that made him successful.

One of Ortega's strengths is that he would go out of his way to find out what the customer genuinely wanted. He also had an eye for trends.

The following is just one famous story about Ortega. He was in his car one day, stopped at a traffic light, and a young man on a motorbike pulled up alongside him. Ortega was so impressed with the fashion statement of the jacket on the motorbike rider that he immediately phoned his company and described the fashion in detail. The company heavily promoted that type of garment and again it was hugely successful.

Ortega ignores the idea that he has the answer to the world's problems and instead concentrates on creating clothing that people genuinely want. As an entrepreneur, you can sometimes focus so much on your creativity that you miss the niche or the problem-solving that your product can provide. A brilliant product that few people want is not nearly as successful as a regular product that is in huge demand.

On speed, Ortega knows that if people see a particular garment, they want it yesterday. Ortega goes out of his way to make sure that the goods people want are immediately available. An excited customer who can't get the product for two to three weeks is a lost customer.

## YOUR GREATEST COMPETITOR IS YOURSELF

One of the most interesting comments about the business Ortega created from scratch is that he seemed to spend very little time worrying about the competition and instead concentrated on his own company's performance. Surely that is a valuable lesson for every entrepreneur. A retail analyst said this of Inditex: "Very few companies can challenge Inditex at this time. The company is in a race with themselves rather than anything else."

## IT'S CALLED THE SNOWBALL BENEFIT

In recent years, the economy of Spain has suffered greatly with crippling debt and 25% unemployment. Despite the economic doom and gloom, Ortega's business continues to thrive. In fact, where many companies have suffered and even gone out of business, Inditex made terrific profits, with a revenue increase of almost 20%. New Zara stores are opening all the time.

How can this relate to you as an entrepreneur? The principle of the snowball rolling down the mountain is that once it's created in the right style and shape and pointed in the right direction, it continues to grow. It gathers speed and power and continues onward, bigger and faster. In some of my businesses I talk about this as momentum and when we start to get it—as a leader—I focus my attention on trying to keep it with the teams, as it's a powerful force.

Why has this happened with the business created by Ortega? He knew well the market in which he was operating. He had experience in the clothing industry from a variety of points of view. He started small and only expanded when he was successful at a certain level.

## FINAL THOUGHT

Of course, we don't have to follow his principles or business model to the letter, but copying some parts works wonderfully well. This is what modelling is all about.

He knew the business from the ground up before

he became an entrepreneur. He didn't need vast amounts of start-up capital because he started small with just one garment, and built a following. Only when he was successful with a single clothing store did he expand, both in the number of stores and in the range of garments. And when he did expand, he did so without putting his business in danger.

As his success continued and his profits accumulated, Ortega spread his investments. Sure, he expanded the empire, but he also put money into other fields such as real estate and energy.

If you have a limited education but a drive to succeed, or if you have limited capital and can find a way to start small, you may be like this humble Spanish man who worked his way up the entrepreneurial ladder to become one of the wealthiest men in the world. He must have done something right, and any part of that could be the inspiration and the motivation to get you and your business off the ground, or flying even higher.

# 10

## STEVE JOBS

Steve Jobs died in 2011. Net worth in 2010: US$10.2 billion.

The technological visionary and his Apple: Steve Jobs

When Steve Jobs passed away in 2011, people around the world mourned. Apple stores set up simple shrines with photographs, and people brought flowers and candles to set beside his pictures. It's rare that an entrepreneur in any business would receive this outpouring of grief. It's a testament to the difference Jobs made in people's lives. He created technologies that captivated users and made their lives better. "It's not a faith in technology," Jobs said, "it's faith in people."

The circumstances of Jobs' early life were difficult. When he was born, his mother, Joanna, and father,

Abdulfatah, were not married. What's more, his maternal grandfather objected to his daughter marrying Steve's father. As a consequence, young Steve was adopted by Paul and Clara Jobs. Throughout his life, Steve Jobs declared that his adoptive parents were his parents. "Paul and Clara are 100% my parents. And Joanna and Abdulfatah are only a sperm and an egg bank. It's not rude, it is the truth."

He did make contact with his birth mother later in life and, in a bizarre fashion, had also met his birth father, although neither knew of the situation. His birth father had become the manager of a California restaurant and had often been heard to boast that he had many high-flying guests, including the computer whiz Steve Jobs, who apparently was a very good tipper. It was Lord Byron who said, "Truth is strange, indeed stranger than fiction."

In looking for adoptive parents, Joanna was adamant that the couple should have a college education just as she and Jobs' father had. It turned out that Mr and Mrs Jobs were not college educated, but Mr Jobs was brilliant with his hands and Mrs Jobs was brilliant with figures. As a result, young Steve was taught to tinker with all sorts of things, and his mother made sure that he was good with calculating and other educational pursuits. There was a time in young Steve's elementary education where teachers recommended he should skip two grades.

As so often happens with great discoveries, the beginning of the Apple Computer saga contained an element of mystery. Steve was not the sole founder or inventor and, in fact, there was another Steve, a man called Steve Wozniak. There was also a third man involved in the beginning and because these young men enjoyed eating apples they decided to call their company Apple. It's a good job they weren't keen on bananas because the Banana Mac just doesn't have the same ring!

There were some other outstanding incidents in the life of Steve Jobs. Having developed Apple Inc. and gone on to become its CEO, he found himself in conflict with the board of management and was, in effect, sacked. He was given a meaningless title and sent to a building that was nearly empty. Being the sort of person he was, Jobs resigned, started another company called NeXTSTEP, and developed what became known as the NeXT Computer.

This computer became so successful that Apple sought to acquire the business, which in turn led to Steve Jobs going back to Apple and finishing up again as its CEO. There's a tale of failure and revival in itself. At the time, Apple was going through a rocky patch and once Jobs got back on board, the company took off. The iPhone, iPod, iPad and iTunes were just some of the fabulously successful products developed by Apple under the stewardship of Jobs.

But that was not all—Jobs was also interested in movies and entertainment, and was a driving force behind the wildly successful animated film company Pixar, which produced such hits as *Toy Story* and *Finding Nemo*. Because of its success, Pixar was bought by the Disney Corporation, making Jobs the largest stockholder in that entertainment giant.

His health issues were widely known, and tragically Jobs died a relatively young man in his mid-50s. Fortunately, there are many aspects of the way he did business that we can learn from.

## HE HAD A PASSION FOR HIS BUSINESS AND HIS PRODUCTS

Are you one of those entrepreneurs who could never picture doing anything other than what you are doing right now? If so, you're just like Steve Jobs.

Millions of people, from time to time, ask themselves whether or not they're in the right job. If you have to ask yourself that question, then you probably are in the wrong one. That wasn't the case with Jobs. He knew what he wanted to do, he loved what he wanted to do, and he did it with a passion.

> 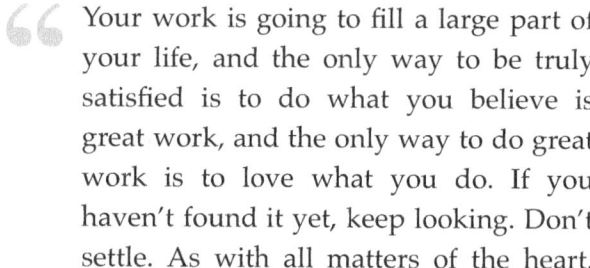 Your work is going to fill a large part of your life, and the only way to be truly satisfied is to do what you believe is great work, and the only way to do great work is to love what you do. If you haven't found it yet, keep looking. Don't settle. As with all matters of the heart, you'll know when you find it.

## CAN YOU BE HARSH?

There are hundreds of stories about how Steve Jobs used to chew out other people. He wasn't shy about being critical. Jobs justified his harshness by saying that you should "be a yardstick of quality". "Some people aren't used to an environment where excellence is expected," he said.

Now, this can be good or bad. If people deserve to be criticised, then it seems right to point out the error of their ways. Allowing someone who is poor or sloppy to continue in a position is bad news for the company's bottom line. The point Jobs would make is that people who are not good performers are actually damaging or holding back the company. If you look upon yourself as a social service, then you will never criticise or sack anyone. What is your approach to criticism of your team?

## CAN YOU CHANGE AND MELLOW?

People who knew Steve Jobs when he first worked for Apple, and then again when he came back, will tell you that while he remained critical, he did mellow. People point out that the reason he changed was because he realised that he couldn't succeed by himself. He needed the support of others. The question here is, can you learn to become a better entrepreneur by becoming a better leader? If you want your business to succeed, then you need to have the people on your side willingly contribute, rather than perform only because they are afraid of criticism. Finding that balance is where Jobs ultimately won.

## BECOME A CUSTOMER

Jobs always looked at his products from the perspective of the customer. "We didn't build the Mac for anybody else," he said. "We built it for ourselves. We were the group of people who were going to judge whether it was great or not."

He had that great knack of being able to ask what somebody would want. If something was too bulky or too expensive or too old-fashioned, then those things needed to change. Having touch-sensitive screens on digital appliances just seemed like a natural thing to do. He could sense or would discover what the customer needed. You need to be in a position to discover what your customers want. Spend time on the receiving end of your products and services.

## PRICE IS ALWAYS A FACTOR

When Jobs first led Apple, and when he moved on to NeXT, the products he produced were expensive—the NeXT computers cost close to US$10,000 per unit. Admittedly they were aimed at the education market, but even so people simply baulked at the price. All the while, Microsoft continued to dominate the market because its products did a good job for a reasonable price. Fast-forward to Jobs' return as the CEO of Apple, and along came the brilliant and relatively cheaper products such as the iPod, the iPhone and the iPad. Jobs had learned that price point is always a factor, and these new and exciting products suddenly came out at a price that many people thought was reasonable. The quality of your products must always be top class, but the price most definitely needs to be competitive.

Does your value perception of your product or service easily exceed the actually cost you're asking? If not, then either add more value or reduce the cost.

## FIND A NEW WAY TO WIN

Unless the products or services you provide are unique, you are in a competition; there are other entrepreneurs doing something very similar. For you to excel, you have to do a number of things. When Steve Jobs returned to Apple, the company was close to bankruptcy. Many competitors made the sorts of things that Apple did. Dell computers removed the middleman in marketing their computers and so were able to sell their products at a cheaper cost. What did Apple do? They opened their own stores. They matched and even beat Dell. There were plenty of mobile phones available, such as the Blackberry, and Jobs didn't try to compete on a like-for-like basis. The Apple iPhone was completely different. The screen was different, the way to operate it was different, and the impact it had on the market was fantastic. Many of the computers being produced at the time were dull as far as colours are concerned. Apple went out of its way to make the actual appearance of the computer a statement in itself.

Are you thinking of context or content first?

## LOOK AFTER YOUR HEALTH

It doesn't matter how clever or how hardworking you are as an entrepreneur, if your health suffers your business will suffer. Perhaps the most important advice we can take from Jobs is that you should at all times look after your health. His unfortunate death from pancreatic cancer was given wide publicity. So too was the fact that when he was originally diagnosed Jobs chose to ignore the advice of the traditional medical world and instead opt for naturopathic solutions.

Usually pancreatic cancer is extremely difficult to beat, but in the case of Jobs, he had a rare form of the disease, one that can be, and has been, successfully treated. Medical opinion seems to be that had Jobs immediately accepted the traditional medical advice and undertaken the treatment they recommended, his chances of beating the cancer would've been better. One can never be absolutely certain of this, but we can at least think about the importance of our own health and wellbeing.

Working extremely hard may improve the bottom line, but if the cost is your own physical or mental health then the cost is too great. Look after yourself.

## NEVER EASE UP

Now having just encouraged you to ensure that your health is your top priority, here comes another lesson from Jobs. Just take a brief look at the Apple history. Shortly before Jobs returned as CEO for the second time, Apple was on its knees. Jobs returned, and about 10 years later Apple was the boom company of the world. A number of its competitors, such as Motorola, Sony and HTC, were suffering big-time. If those companies had been in a war, they would have waved the white flag to Apple. What a time for Apple to gloat, relax, and spend the profits.

But Apple didn't do that, and just as well. Samsung and Google were already building up a powerful reputation. Now we know how powerful those two businesses have become, yet Apple is still a major player. Why? Because Apple has never taken its foot off the accelerator. The company continues to look for new ideas and for new ways to improve its products. We're at a point where the next iPhone receives almost saturation media coverage, with devoted consumers spending the night outside their local Apple store wanting to be one of the first to get the latest product. You can never take your mind off the task of continuing to improve and continuing to excel.

Who are you chasing, even when you're winning? When I travel I always choose to sit in the second row of the plane, so I'm always reminded that there is someone to chase. What's something you do to remind yourself of your victories? Or to remind yourself that someone out there is chasing your tail, or is ahead of you?

THE STEAK AND THE SIZZLE

One of the things Steve Jobs was particularly good at was selling the brand and the concept. Of course, you have to have an excellent product or service in the first place, but let's assume you have. You still can't succeed unless you can sell it. If you look at the way Jobs used to give a sales presentation for the latest Apple product, you will never find a comparable approach.

The fact that he wore the same casual clothes and adopted a laid-back approach to addressing the media was super-important. His opponents or competitors couldn't understand why Apple got so much publicity. Of course, the products were brilliant, but the way they were presented by their CEO was a brilliant piece of selling. He had the build-up, the crowd, the secretive lead-up to the unveiling, the packaging, the whole company at launches, the movie-like trailer video and he 'owned' the stage.

The famous circus owner PT Barnum knew all about show business and the art of attracting customers to his performances. Steve Jobs was not unlike Barnum. As somebody once said, it's not much good having the steak if you haven't got the sizzle. What can you do to add sizzle to your business?

## ARE YOU A PUSH-DOWN ENTREPRENEUR?

The way that Apple has become so successful is due to its push-down policy as far as responsibility is concerned. Rather than give all of the power to one or two people at the apex of the pyramid, Apple pushes down responsibility to a range of managers below the top level. Each of these managers has a specific task and is responsible for that task.

There are far too many stories of businesses where the leader is out of touch with reality, or that create bottlenecks with over-involved management or owners. Apple is very clever in this regard because with full responsibility given to a group of managers throughout the entire operation, it's very hard for the entire operation to get into trouble. Could you make each person on your team more responsible for company outcomes by helping them to 'own' their particular area?

The bigger the company, obviously the greater the need for this push-down of responsibility, but the principle applies regardless of the size of your operation. Allow others to be responsible.

### FINAL THOUGHT

Steve Jobs barely needs an introduction. Chances are if you're not holding this book you're reading or listening to it on one of his devices. Jobs was a unique visionary who didn't just create a successful company, he changed people's lives for the better through technology. He did this on his terms, whether it was by dressing in the casual way he wanted or by producing technology he would buy if he were a customer.

Jobs' untimely death didn't end Apple either—his vision and way of doing things were so ingrained in the DNA of the company that Apple's new CEO, Tim Cook, and long-time designer Jonathan I've have been able to continue to keep the company moving forward. With cash reserves at nearly $180 billion and visionaries at the top, Apple shows no signs of slowing down. Jobs will be long remembered for reaching customers' hearts as well as their minds, through Apple products.

In the words of Jobs himself, "Here's to the crazy ones". (Yes, he's talking about you.)

## 11

## ARIANNA HUFFINGTON

Arianna Huffington lives in California, USA. Current net worth: US$35 million.

Mind, body, and soul: Arianna Huffington's advice for entrepreneurs

Typical entrepreneurship advice tends to begin and end with a focus on tactics or strategies. Arianna Huffington—noted author, political commentator, and founder of *The Huffington Post*—argues that entrepreneurs should also focus on their own health and wellness. It sounds like 'no-brainer' advice, but it's an important note for hardworking entrepreneurs. Giving time for yourself away from the business can, paradoxically, translate into a more productive person and workplace. Huffington is a great believer that if you look after number one you become much better at looking after others.

In 2014, *Forbes* magazine described Huffington as

the 52nd most powerful woman in the world. Born in Athens, Greece, in 1950, Huffington was educated at Cambridge University in England and subsequently became an extremely successful businesswoman in the United States. After becoming a naturalised American citizen in 1990, she ran for the post of governor of California in 2003. Soon afterwards, she started *The Huffington Post*, which rapidly became a popular online news website. In 2011, she sold *The Huffington Post* for more than $300 million.

Let's look at Huffington's often-overlooked holistic advice for entrepreneurs.

## FOCUS ON THE WHOLE SELF

Do you work like a dog or do you know when to stop and recharge your batteries? Huffington notes that great entrepreneurs such as Bill Gates and Steve Jobs often simply walked away from their business to rest and recharge. Are you going to work day after day, never giving your mind and body a chance to break from that routine? By going to a completely different environment and by taking your mind away from the decisions you were making, you give your business the boost it needs. Huffington most certainly believes in this adage: *a change is as good as a holiday*.

Working hard is good, and many entrepreneurs will tell you it's essential. However, working too hard without any recharge points is a major no-no. "We think, mistakenly," Huffington says, "that success is the result of the amount of time we put in at work, instead of the quality of time we put in."

Overwork causes people to self-medicate to deal with the stress and pain—how many painkillers do you take, or how many beers do you drink after a tough day? Huffington tells us that medication is just a way for the body to tell us that we need to slow down. If you're in your 40s or 50s and needing medical attention for stress-related illness, then Huffington calls this a flashing neon sign telling you to slow down. Being successful is never worth your health.

And on the same issue of health, sleep is vitally important to the Huffington lifestyle. Huffington is bold about the importance of sleep:

> Sleep deprivation reduces our emotional intelligence, self-regard, assertiveness, sense of independence, empathy toward others, the quality of our interpersonal relationships, positive thinking, and impulse control. Everything you do, you'll do better with a good night's sleep.

Setting up nap rooms in her workplaces, she wrote a book cleverly titled *How to Sleep Your Way to the Top*. She's a great believer in plenty of restful sleep and even recommends topping up with an extra 30 minutes just so your energy levels are at their absolute best for the entire day.

Another practice from the self-help books that Huffington promotes is meditation, which she calls a "reboot for your brain and your soul". To some people, meditation is a complete waste of time. To others, it's the perfect way to start a new day. Steve Jobs of Apple fame believed he got his best ideas after meditating. Why not look at some simple ways to try meditation before you start each day? It may well be the case of less haste, more speed.

Some entrepreneurs direct their eyes to a digital device on a constant basis. Huffington advocates a change. She believes that by operating a number of devices you are actually becoming unproductive. You need to stop looking at the screen and start looking at your workplace and your work colleagues. By all means take advantage of the great qualities of digital devices, but never let them rule your life.

What we produce for the world begins within. When we understand our own mind, when we are at peace with ourselves, we are in the ideal position to do things that are noticed by the outside world. The outside world judges us by what we say and do. Huffington believes that to perfect what we say and do, we need to perfect ourselves on the inside.

## GIVING, NOT TAKING

Huffington is a strong advocate of the law of reciprocity—she believes most definitely in the adage that it is far better to give than to receive. Think of networking: many people look at networking as a way to get something. She advocates that you look at networking from a different point of view. Instead, think about what you can give others. All of this flows into her belief that if you remove the word 'competition' and substitute 'collaboration', you're well on the way to not just making a difference but making a *significant* difference.

In this vein, Huffington likes to channel the Dalai Lama's attitudes and practices, trying to bring gratitude into her life. Have you considered the possibility that if you change your lifestyle—if you become more positive and have a genuine appreciation of the worth and value of other people, be they your fellow workers or clients—that change in your attitude will reflect in your role as an entrepreneur?

It's very easy to get upset at any number of people. It could be your business partner, one of your team, a customer, or even one of your suppliers. Huffington believes that if you want to slow down your creativity, and thus your productivity, then you should hold on to those grudges. She sees holding a grudge as drinking poison. Your energy levels are reduced and the difficulty of being successful becomes even harder. Her solution is to promote generosity, forgiveness and humbleness. For many people, it's just too hard to do both, but Huffington is an example of practising what you preach, and that sounds like pretty good advice.

## OPENNESS

Make yourself available. Huffington is not the only hugely successful entrepreneur to do this, but she freely gives out her email address. If you wish to write to her, you can. You would think that somebody of her wealth and status and position would not want to be bothered by people badgering her or requesting all types of things.

## THE RIGHT ENVIRONMENT

Is your workplace a happy one? Huffington is a great believer in restructuring the workplace. She thinks about other things too, but of primary concern is the setup and environment in which her fellow workers operate. Her comment is that we need to find the joy in what we're doing. The relevance of this and the beauty of this is that the better the environment of your workplace, the greater the benefits for all. Your staff members are more productive and far more likely to want to stay within your organisation.

I love this idea, and for as long as I can remember I've always had my teams sit and work around giant tables together, not at separate desks facing the walls! What could you do in your office?

## FEAR OF FAILURE

Many entrepreneurs worry about failure. Having spoken to hundreds of thousands of budding entrepreneurs over the years—and being one myself—I can tell you that it takes guts and certainly a lot of planning to make a success of your ideas. Rather than looking at failure as a weakness, Huffington regards it as a stepping-stone towards becoming successful. Huffington says, "You have to do what you dream of doing even while you're afraid." She believes that you have to accept the fact that failure is a reality, although you should do everything to avoid it. If it does happen, use it as a way of picking yourself up, improving and doing things better. Huffington argues that "failure is not the opposite of success, it's part of success".

## STANDING UP FOR BELIEFS

Whatever else you may say about Arianna Huffington, you can never accuse her of being silent on her opinions. *The Huffington Post* is a perfect example of this. Huffington has long been a strong advocate for causes in which she has a passionate belief. She believes that to be a great leader or entrepreneur, you need to have the courage to stand up for your beliefs. The great leaders she admires are those who have a vision and values, and who are prepared to do as much as humanly and reasonably possible to achieve their goals. Yes, they will receive criticism and misunderstanding and whatever else comes their way for being a strong leader, but if you wish to be successful, you need to be bold in telling the world what you think and getting people to pay attention.

## FINAL THOUGHT

Arguably the top lesson we can learn from Huffington's success is to focus on the bigger picture. All the professional planning and preparation for a successful business should never supplant the need for developing the right philosophy and inspiring vision.

This begins with her belief in looking after number one. While she advocates that giving is always better than receiving, she never loses sight of her number-one goal, which is to make sure she is fit and well, in order to succeed as an entrepreneur.

The path to success as an entrepreneur is paved with ups and downs, and our abilities to centre our emotional, physical and spiritual wellness in order to be strong enough to stand the tides is paramount.

## 12

## INGVAR KAMPRAD

Ingvar Kamprad lives in Sweden. Current net worth: US$23 billion.

Assembling a furniture empire.

Born in Sweden in 1926, Ingvar Kamprad made his billions from a simple concept: inexpensive, simple furniture you assemble yourself. You probably have purchased a side table or a desk from his now-famous company, IKEA. The letters of IKEA are actually a combination of Kamprad's first and last name, and the name of the village and farm where he grew up. From that village to the world, IKEA now has hundreds of stores in dozens of countries. Kamprad explains that, "It was our duty to expand. Those who cannot or will not join us are to be pitied. What we want to do, we can do and will do, together. A glorious future!"

Kamprad became self-employed at a surprisingly young age, because he knew how to take the initiative.

As a young boy, he regularly hopped on his bicycle and rode to his neighbours, offering to sell them matches. He had already worked out that he could buy them in bulk and make a handy profit by selling them in small amounts. He asked his aunt to purchase them for him when she travelled into Stockholm.

But it wasn't only matches—as a young boy he also sold such things as Christmas-tree decorations, fish he caught, and berries he picked, as well as pens and pencils, all while he continued his studies. When he finished high school at age 17, his father gave him a cash reward for being successful. He used some of this seed money to start what has become one of the most successful furniture-manufacturing and retailing businesses in the world.

IKEA literally began on a kitchen table as a mail-order operation. Convenience is a major drawcard for customers, and if you have a great product that is hard to buy or collect, you will always lose out to the entrepreneur who has service as a top priority.

## SELLING LEADERSHIP

Kamprad was brilliant at selling, even as a child. As an entrepreneur, it's easily one of the most important skills. There are so many ways you can improve your selling technique and skill set, and apply it to use within your business. What we're really talking about is influence and persuasion, and what you can do with it. Of course, the obvious is that you can sell your product or service if you're skilled, but what about using the skills to convince someone to join your company? Or foster loyalty within your team, convincing them that you are a great leader and open to ideas? If you are passionate about the goods or services you produce, you naturally sell them better. "What is good for our customers is also, in the long run, good for us," Kamprad says.

Throughout his life, Kamprad has given advice that he has put into practice himself. His passion and enthusiasm for his products shine through. His attitude of 'don't do what I say but do as I do' encourages people to believe in him and makes him an ideal selling leader and one adept at constantly selling his vision.

## KNOWING WHAT'S IMPORTANT

Despite being a billionaire, Kamprad has long believed in being frugal. Until quite recently, Kamprad lived in Switzerland, drove a 1993 Volvo, and pocketed condiment packages in restaurants.

When he first started IKEA, Kamprad was so passionate about the business that he devoted almost his entire life to it. Later, he had some regrets, wondering if he missed out on good times as a young man. Many of his friends would go out on social occasions and enjoy a beer or three while he was at home, building furniture. Some say that he bought a Porsche to remind himself of his absent youth.

As the years rolled by, Kamprad realised that despite his huge personal wealth, his personal happiness came from living a simple life and being successful at what he did. A good lesson here is that he didn't pay attention to what people said about him. Whether you are frugal or flashy, or somewhere in between, it's important that you are happy in your own skin.

With a company founder who still encourages employees to write on both sides of all pieces of paper, it's no wonder that IKEA continues to prosper. Making money is always a priority but cutting costs helps profit grow and keep growing. "People say I am cheap," Kamprad says, "and I don't mind if they do. How the hell can I tell people who work for me to travel cheaply when I travel in luxury? It's a question of good leadership."

Do you have actions you dislike? From an early age, Kamprad disliked borrowing money. This drove him to rarely do so, to work much harder, thus to not be in a position where he needed other people's money. What is important to you?

ARE YOU A BELIEVER?

As an entrepreneur, it's important to have faith in your idea. In business, as in life, there is often no such thing as a sure thing. You have an idea and you carry out due diligence, you do all of the marketing and testing you can think of, but there is still no cast-iron guarantee that what you hope to happen will happen. However, the difference between good and great entrepreneurs is that those who are great have an idea, and have the drive and desire to see it through.

When Kamprad started IKEA, he could not survive as a small operator, as there were already many furniture manufacturers and retailers. He was not breaking new ground. He did, however, believe in giving each product a distinct name rather than simply a catalogue number. People saw that approach as unique.

Following World War II, home delivery was not a new concept, but Kamprad decided to have a combination of bricks-and-mortar stores as well as delivery by post. Offering both was a masterstroke. People could go to the physical store and handle the products. They could sit on the beds or the chairs. They could open the cupboards and drawers. They could see the quality of the manufacture, and they could make price comparisons. If they wanted to, then they could purchase the products and take them home with them, or they could have them delivered. Kamprad believed in his products and in his idea of offering an all-round service.

## TOO MANY EGGS IN YOUR BASKET

Over the years, I've echoed the sentiment 'Inch Wide, Mile Deep', imploring entrepreneurs to find a niche that they could dominate. When IKEA began, it sold a number of things, including watches and Christmas cards. After a few years, Kamprad dispensed with any product that wasn't related to furniture. Interior design was to be the sole focus.

Today you can go into a massive IKEA store or thumb through a huge IKEA catalogue and you will see nothing but interior decoration and furniture. By becoming a specialist, IKEA boomed. Do you have too many eggs in your basket? Is it possible for you to drop some of the activities you are currently doing and concentrate on only one thing? Would you be better at that one thing if that was all you had to worry about? This is the same approach Steve Jobs had when he took back the reins at Apple, and now the rest is history.

## CHOCOLATES AT THE CHECKOUT

The reason that many supermarkets put tasty treats close to the cash register is that they hope people will simply top up their grocery supplies with low-cost, pleasurable products. Retailers also hope that begging children will persuade their parents to grab a chocolate bar.

IKEA has a simple and unique philosophy when it comes to selling food within its store. Anyone who has sat in an IKEA restaurant knows that the food prices are quite low. There is method to the IKEA madness. If people spend time in an IKEA store, they may become hungry, but they don't have to leave the store to enjoy a coffee, or even dinner. That thinking may well keep those people in the store longer and therefore they may spend more.

IKEA is also open to new approaches. They sold Christmas trees and promised to buy back the tree if the customer came back after Christmas with the product. They gave away a single shoe in a pair of wooden shoes and promised they would give the customer the other shoe if the customer came back. Are you thinking along these outside-the-box marketing ideas? On the surface, it may seem that the company gives away too much, but this marketing philosophy of doing the unusual keeps the customer coming back.

## DON'T BE AFRAID OF MAKING A MISTAKE

Mistakes are a part of life; and definitely a part of business. The key is to learn from your mistake, to not repeat it, and to benefit from the added knowledge. "Only those who are asleep make no mistakes. There are few people who have made so many fiascos in life as I have," says Kamprad. Now there's a confession! A billionaire who built a global company from scratch, openly saying that he has made more mistakes than almost anyone else.

IKEA lost millions by investing in the manufacture and sale of television sets. Kamprad tried to get his business going in Russia and ran up against the bureaucracy—that little venture cost him millions. He lost a lot of money through a factory that failed in Romania. And then IKEA opened a store in the wrong city. The boss wanted Koblenz, but a staff member thought he said Konstanz and yes, if you can believe it, the store opened in the wrong place!

It's important that you are prepared to take risks and not be afraid of failure. Naturally, Kamprad took as many steps possible, as far as due diligence was concerned. But having made mistakes, he was not deterred from moving forward with new ideas and new developments. The strength of IKEA today is testament to his willingness to have a go.

Mistakes may not come only in the operation of the

business but also in one's private life. A difficult tale in Kamprad's past has recently come under public scrutiny. His ancestors on his father's side came from Germany, and as a teenager in the 1940s, when the world was at war, Kamprad joined a pro-fascist political movement. In 2011, when a journalist reported on his early political leanings, Kamprad came out and declared his affiliation with the fascist organisation to be "the greatest mistake of my life".

## LEARN HOW TO FIGHT HARD

IKEA's great success made many of its competitors unhappy, and many furniture manufacturers refused to deal with the company. Kamprad was banned from attending exhibitions and even had to create false companies in order to continue doing business, because the name IKEA turned off so many people in the industry. Kamprad never gave up though. The fact that he kept fighting only added to his status as a hero to many people, including those in his team and the buying public

The consequence of not working with IKEA, however, was a big one: other manufacturers were forced to learn how to design their own furniture. They then had to source raw material from countries outside of Sweden. Had his competitors cooperated and supported IKEA, everyone would've been a winner. As it turned out, the greatest winner was Kamprad and IKEA.

## FINAL THOUGHT

IKEA has done a number of unusual things, from its furniture concept to its marketing and store layout, leading a revolution in the retail industry. Every time it came up against opposition, it found a way to go out on a limb and overcome the problem.

IKEA has never been a publicly owned company. Kamprad has taken the point of view that if you hand over your company to shareholders, they can do a number of disagreeable things. They can force you to make profit far more important than it needs to be, and they can force you to change the direction of the company.

When IKEA first began in America, its rate of growth was exceptionally slow. Many commentators felt that it could never prosper, but Kamprad and IKEA were in it for the long haul, and patience is a virtue. They succeeded in America as they have succeeded everywhere.

# 13

## CARLOS SLIM

Carlos Slim lives in Mexico City. Current net worth: US$55.7 billion.

### Slim by name, fat by wealth: think like Carlos Slim

Mexico has produced many great soccer players like Hugo Sánchez, Rafael Márquez, and Javier Hernández, but it has not produced many billionaires. Yet Mexican Carlos Slim has often topped the list of the world's wealthiest men.

Well-versed in the vagaries of economics, Slim invested heavily in cut-price industries when the Mexican economy suffered significant hardship in the early 1980s. He owned almost a 50% interest in the Mexican branches of the Hershey Company and British American Tobacco. Buying businesses in an economic downturn meant that he got them for a cheap price and then, when the economy picked up, the value of his assets improved remarkably.

Slim is known to diversify his holdings. In the late 80s and early 90s, Slim became a keen investor in communication companies. He made a bold purchase of a telephone company in Mexico that controlled 90% of the country's telephone lines. Further investment meant that his company controlled almost 80% of cell phones in Mexico. Since then, Slim has invested heavily in a chain of hotels as well as in other media companies. He even became a partner with Microsoft via a Spanish portal that operated in his homeland.

The fifth of six children, Slim has a family story that sounds like the clichéd American Dream. His parents were born in Lebanon, but they migrated to Mexico in the early 20th century. His wife's parents also migrated to Mexico. They brought a printing press with them and published one of the first Arabic newspapers in Mexico. Carlos' father bought real estate in Mexico City and the value of this property greatly appreciated. Born into a wealthy family, Slim studied civil engineering at university in Mexico.

Slim's father taught him and his siblings the basics of operating a business. By the age of 12, Slim was the proud owner of shares in a Mexican bank. His father offered him employment, but Slim chose to work as a stockbroker in Mexico and from there went on to form his own brokerage firm. This gave him inside knowledge about various aspects of business and which areas of business were likely to prosper.

As well as advising his clients on which shares to purchase, he began to purchase shares himself. His choice of shares meant his portfolio became varied and solid. His investment career continued to bloom, and before long he purchased successful companies and formed a corporation as an umbrella company in order to house his many investments. At first, his interests were in real estate, mining and construction, but in time he moved into other areas such as printing, retailing, food and tobacco.

Now let's look at some of the guiding principles in Slim's business life.

## COMPETENCIES

The reason Slim came to be so successful and maintain that success was because he followed these three principles:

- He understood the business of business
- He was willing to cooperate with his competitors
- He looked at the market as being local, national and international.

Slim believes that people can be good with words and can communicate well, and that people can also be good with figures—they can understand a balance sheet and know what is happening within their company or companies. If you do not have a grasp of numbers, then you don't have a grasp of your company. "If you're in business, you need to understand the environment. You need to have a vision of the future, and you need to know the past," Slim says.

Do not look upon your competitors as enemies. While

we tend to think of competition as taking something from us, Slim makes a unique point: "Competition makes you better, always… even if the competitor wins." Also, there may be ways in which you can cooperate. If it means that both of you prosper, then that has to be worthwhile.

While it is important to find customers locally, it is also important to look for customers elsewhere in the world. Slim calls this "an international reference". This reference point provides perspective on the industry and ideas for change and expansion.

In our 'global village' that is business in the 21st century, going global can be easier than it looks.

## PAY ATTENTION TO THE ECONOMIC CIRCUMSTANCES

Decide what your core business is all about. As an entrepreneur, you may not be interested in becoming a collector of companies as Carlos Slim is. But it is possible that you can acquire another business similar to yours. Whatever you do, however, you must be firm in your knowledge regarding your core business. Never lose sight of the reason for creating your business in the first place. Be open and consider other options, but never change horses mid-stream.

One of the best times to make a takeover bid is when the economy is heading south. Slim says there are two principles regarding major business moves:

- Make your move when others are moving out

- Always have a plan ready to make a significant move.

Making decisions on the run can be fraught with danger at times, when it comes to investing. Think about what you could be doing in a new business move, even if you are not planning to do it in the immediate future. If the circumstances warrant it, have a plan and capital ready to go. And when economic times are tough, this can be the best time to make a powerful move; just like in the real estate industry.

Over many decades Slim has acquired hundreds of companies. He always buys when he believes he is able to improve the purchased company and turn it into a more profitable operation. But he does not hesitate to sell if he believes it is the right thing to do. There can be any number of reasons why he would sell a particular company, but certainly the principle of never selling does not apply. For any entrepreneur, the lesson here is that you should not become set in your ways, and look to expand. I've always believed that when things are going well is the time to leverage and grow into new markets, which is the principle we follow in our investment business Paragon Global Investments.

## BECOME A GOOD CORPORATE CITIZEN

Like many hugely successful entrepreneurs, Carlos Slim is an outstanding benefactor. Slim has a dedicated program to look for causes that he and his colleagues believe are worthy of support, and then donate accordingly. He is also very involved in education and provides many scholarships for students every year. "It's important to give a better country to your children," he says, "but it is more important to give better children to your country."

If you are a beginning entrepreneur you may not be in a position to make massive donations to worthy causes. However, it can be an excellent idea for you, even a as a small-time entrepreneur, to think about your role as a good corporate citizen. Associating yourself with the support of local charities or providing scholarships for children in need can make you and your business feel good, and it can also promote the quality and good name of your business in the community.

## POVERTY IS AN OPPORTUNITY FOR WEALTH CREATION

Mexico has significant pockets of poverty, but Slim believes the problem isn't solved only with donations. "Our concept is more to accomplish and solve things, rather than giving; that is, not going around like Santa Claus," he says. Slim regards this hardship as an opportunity for economic development. He sees it as a challenge to use his companies and the ability of these companies to grow, linked to the needs of so many people in poverty. If his companies can prosper, they can offer employment opportunities to more and more people. A recent survey showed that the Slim companies employed approximately a quarter of a million people. The more success his companies have, the more employees they can take on board, and the more they can help reduce poverty in the country.

## DON'T BRING ME PROBLEMS, BRING ME SOLUTIONS

In Mexico and in the world of business, there will always be problems and challenges. Slim thrives on these situations, and rather than becoming depressed and worried about what can be done, he regards the problem as a solution. The situation is not one of hardship but rather one of a challenge. This is a hugely helpful attitude.

As an entrepreneur, you will undoubtedly encounter problems. If you can switch your attitude and reframe your mind to thinking that a problem is an opportunity for you to excel, to do the right thing by your work colleagues and your customers, then you will be a far better entrepreneur. A major turnaround in the fortunes of your business life can take place simply because of a major turnaround in your attitudes. The next problem that arises in your day-to-day job can suddenly become an opportunity for you to discover a way to fix it, to become a better entrepreneur, and to boost your bottom line. Challenge equals opportunity.

Where are the 'opportunities' in your life right now?

## LESSONS IN LIFE

Because of his extraordinary wealth and position of influence in society, Slim takes seriously the role he can play in influencing other people; particularly young people. In 1994, he published an open letter to outstanding university students. Some sections of this open letter reveal a great deal about the man and his attitude to business and to life. Here's his philosophy of success:

> Success is not about doing things well or even very well, or being acknowledged by others. It is the harmony between the soul and your emotions which requires love, family, friendship, authenticity and integrity.

Not exactly the words of the typical wealth-building businessman, are they? In fact, it's just the opposite, as Carlos Slim went on to say the following:

> When you give, do not expect to receive. Do not allow negative feelings and emotions to control your mind. Emotional harm does not come from others; it is conceived and developed within ourselves.

It may come as a surprise that these words were written by a man who was recently the wealthiest person on the planet, buying and selling companies. But he also said the following:

> Do not mix up your values or betray your principles. Life's road is very long,

but it is travelled fast. Live the present intensely and fully, do not let the past be a burden, and let the future be an incentive. Each person forges his or her own destiny and it may influence reality. Do not ignore it.

## FINAL THOUGHT

It is difficult to imagine the wealth that Carlos Slim has obtained. True, his father was successful in business and gave all of his children an education in wealth generation. Despite the enormous entrepreneurial success of Slim, his advice could not be more pointed and appropriate.

He doesn't talk about profit and wealth creation. He talks about developing your life as a person, about being happy and healthy in your own skin, and about giving as opposed to getting.

Of course, Slim has advice on the practical side of business, but so much of what he says is about the passion, not the profits. Making money is fine, desirable, and even necessary, but it is not the primary focus of your activities. Focus on your passion, the drive to build your business. If you do that and you learn the necessary systems and strategies of doing business, then the moneymaking will take care of itself. It's when we find our purpose and live it with passion that the profits roll in!

# 14

## MARK ZUCKERBERG

Mark Zuckerberg lives in Palo Alto, USA. Current net worth: US$56.7 billion.

Making his mark, one computer at a time.

Mark Zuckerberg, born in 1984, is an American computer programmer who studied at Harvard University and created a simple website that quickly became the pre-eminent way to connect human beings in the Digital Age. The story of this website was told in the Hollywood movie *The Social Network*; that website is Facebook.com. In just over 10 years, those social connections have created a company with over US$12 billion in revenues from almost 1.5 billion users around the globe. Yet as founder Mark Zuckerberg says, "Facebook was not originally created to be a company. It was built to accomplish the social mission —to make the world more open and connected."

As Zuckerberg's example shows, big things can

come out of little ideas. Friends enjoying a meal or a coffee together can unwittingly suggest something that could later turn into a brilliant and major project. Things said in jest can become serious business opportunities.

In college, Zuckerberg created a crude dating site for friends, called FaceMash. This very basic website was set up in just one weekend. By Monday, the university had closed it down because its popularity was slowing the campus Internet service. Zuckerberg dropped out of Harvard after his newly named Facebook website took off. "I literally coded Facebook in my dorm room and launched it from my dorm room. I rented a server for $85 a month, and I funded it by putting an ad on the site," he explains.

It's fair to say that Zuckerberg didn't plan to create a billion-dollar company:

> My goal was never to just create a company. A lot of people misinterpret that, as if I don't care about revenue or profit or any of those things. But what not being just a company means to me is not being just that—building something that actually makes a really big change in the world.

Nonetheless, Facebook's quick success meant he and his colleagues were faced with having to make a decision about selling the business. Whenever an idea takes root and becomes wildly successful, it's only natural that investors will arrive with cheque book in hand. Zuckerberg and his partners resisted overtures from AOL and Microsoft, deciding to make a go of it themselves.

This 'mission' has created Zuckerberg's personal wealth of somewhere north of US$56 billion dollars, and yet as the CEO of Facebook he earns a pittance—he takes a one-dollar salary annually. He's won numerous awards and is much in demand as a speaker. Without his work to establish Facebook, you could argue that the world would never have heard of him—but they also would never have connected with so many friends and colleagues either. It's been a symbiotic relationship.

When we talk about great musicians, like Mozart, the word 'prodigy' is often used. As a young boy, Zuckerberg was a digital prodigy, learning computer-programming skills from his father. However, it wasn't long before his father gave up and called in a professional software developer to keep up with his son. While many kids, his age were playing computer games, Zuckerberg was designing them.

Even though Zuckerberg is still young, he has many insights about business for entrepreneurs to learn from. Let's look at some principles behind his Facebook success.

## DO YOU HAVE A HIGHER PURPOSE?

Sometimes an entrepreneur can get caught up in simply selling products or services to others for a fee, but the Facebook story shows that business success comes from thinking more broadly. "Building a mission and building a business go hand-in-hand," says Zuckerberg. This means that while profit isn't a dirty word, the fixation on generating sales can cause you to forget the importance of a social mission.

In the case of Facebook, the social mission—connecting people to other people—is good for business too. Is it possible that in operating your business you are also able to incorporate a social mission like Zuckerberg? And if you can, will that social mission complement your business mission and make both successful?

Zuckerberg recently extended his mission by working with major phone and network infrastructure companies to create Internet. org, an organisation that will bring Internet service to those without the financial means to access it. While this project helps Facebook's business, it also helps underprivileged people receive the same benefits of the Internet that the rest of us take for granted.

## DON'T BE AFRAID TO BREAK THINGS

Zuckerberg is open and frank about the mistakes he and Facebook have made, particularly in the early years. He also points to these mistakes as being wonderful learning tools. "Move fast and break things," he says.

Not all mistakes are created equal, however. Zuckerberg calls some 'false positive mistakes'. Facebook is always upgrading and changing its design, features, and polices, and it often receives complaints from customers about these changes. He describes a false positive mistake as something that at first glance is a mistake, but over time, the change is forgotten and accepted.

The argument put forward by Zuckerberg is that the best way to learn is to tackle something. If it works, then that's fine, but if it doesn't work, then that too can be fine because you have learned from that experience. This is a new experience for many entrepreneurs because you are thinking on your feet; you are reacting in real time.

## ARE YOU AFRAID TO TAKE A RISK?

Do you have the courage to tackle something risky? Zuckerberg has a very simple philosophy on the issue of taking risks: "The biggest risk is not taking any risk."

If you're not afraid to break things, you don't have an option when it comes to avoiding risk. If you are going to be bold and tackle work with enthusiasm, chances are you will experience failure at some point. In the technology business, risk-taking is even more important. Technology changes on an almost daily basis, and if you choose to stand still, that strategy is a risk in itself—you risk being left behind.

Google Buzz and Google Wave were risks and could arguably be described as failures. When Coca-Cola decided to introduce New Coke, they were met with massive resistance. Each of these organisations survived and moved on, taking a new direction.

## YOU NEED TO BUILD A TEAM

One of Zuckerberg's great strengths is his ability to know what he is good at and what he is not good at. From the early days of Facebook, he surrounded himself with quality people who could do the sorts of things that he couldn't do. He wasn't a booted-and-suited executive, even wearing hoodies to executive meetings.

Zuckerberg reckons that he spends about a quarter of his time on recruiting. He is very specific about the type of person he wants to employ and first looks for employees within the Facebook organisation before looking outside.

Zuckerberg puts strong emphasis on choosing the right people not just from an experience and expertise point of view, but also from a vision point of view. He believes it's no good attracting people who may be brilliant at a particular aspect of running a company, but don't share the goals and mission statement of the company. "People can be really smart or have skills that are directly applicable, but if they don't really believe in it, then they are not going to really work hard," he says. This means that you may pass on a potential employee who seems like a great fit for the job description, but who doesn't share the same values as the CEO and his or her fellow executives.

The first step in hiring people with vision, of course, is to have values, a vision, and a mission statement of your own. First, be clear on your mission, and then follow Zuckerberg's example by following it from the first hire—don't wait to become a big company.

## HOW TO HIRE THE RIGHT PEOPLE

"You should aim to get the best people together and align their incentives around doing something great," Zuckerberg says. This sounds right, but how do his hiring principles work in practice? You're sitting opposite somebody, a potential employee of Facebook, and you ask a series of questions and engage in a dialogue. All of this is helpful in assessing the person, their skills, and their values. But is there a much more direct and simple way of deciding whether or not this person is right for your business?

Zuckerberg uses an elementary tactic. He asks himself the following question: "Would I be happy to work for this person?" In other words, he turns the situation around: the interviewer becomes the interviewee. He assesses the person he's interviewing from the point of view of the job applicant. Would this person make a good boss? Would I be happy working for this person, and if so, why?

This all goes back to looking upon your enterprise as a movement or mission, rather than a business that exists purely to make money. Of course, it is a business and, yes, profit is the driving force behind it, but by thinking of this business as a project or as a mission with a vision, your whole attitude towards going to work and being at work takes on a new meaning.

There are two other interesting characteristics Zuckerberg finds essential when hiring people. The person you hire needs to be better or smarter than you are, or an expert in one particular area. Don't choose a jack of all trades, rather a specialist who is the best in the business.

FINAL THOUGHT

Whatever you may think of Mark Zuckerberg and his business philosophy, you cannot question his success. If you want to look at Facebook simply as a start-up enterprise, then it has been a chart-topping monster. That alone entitles its creator to both a platform and our attention.

Perhaps he doesn't speak as a typical CEO may speak, but that is because he isn't a typical CEO. Some people say he isn't a CEO at all. One thing is for sure, he's a very successful entrepreneur who comes at business from a different point of view.

Zuckerberg is very open about his mistakes and about the way he operates. He preaches loud and long the value and importance of surrounding yourself with the right people, and he goes into great detail about who he means by the right people. Thinking about risk-taking, and having a social goal as well as a financial goal are two major cornerstones of how he operates.

# 15

## HOWARD SCHULTZ

Howard Schultz lives in New York, USA. Current net worth: US$3 billion.

No mere bean counter: the inspired leadership of Howard Schultz

Howard Schultz is a perfect example of a rags-to-riches story. Living in Brooklyn, New York, his family was poor and his father, who had little education and drove a delivery truck, died while Howard was a small child. Nobody in Schultz's family had ever been to college.

"I was scarred at a young age with understanding what it was like to watch my parents lose access to the American Dream," Schultz says. With this experience driving him forward, Schultz turned everything around, winning a college football scholarship, owning a professional basketball team, and most importantly, running the biggest coffee-shop company in the world, Starbucks.

Schultz started his business career on the lowest rung, selling homewares and kitchen equipment. Yet selling coffee machines—very successfully as it turned out—was the perfect platform for his future business venture. He moved from his native New York and joined Starbucks in 1982, as director of operations and marketing, when Starbucks had only four stores. After working at Starbucks for a while, he travelled. On his travels in Italy, he fell in love not only with the coffee beans, but also the way Italians sold coffee. He saw how businesses operated in other countries and was very impressed with the espresso coffee shops in Italy.

When he returned to the United States, he tried to persuade Starbucks to emulate the Italians. He tried to convince them that simply selling coffee beans was only part of the job; they could create a much more profitable and interesting business by actually selling coffee drinks. Unfortunately, they didn't share his enthusiasm and weren't interested in his idea.

With this roadblock in his way, Schultz started his own coffee business to compete against Starbucks, called Il Giornale, the name of an Italian newspaper. Howard's coffee business offered better options for customers than Starbucks did, although his business was much smaller.

Il Giornale became so successful that in the late 1980s he was able to purchase his old employer, the Starbucks Company, for approximately US$4 million. When he first started, he was like many would-be entrepreneurs—he lacked the necessary start-up capital. But because of his energy, drive, and vision, Schultz persuaded a number of backers to help him raise the US$400,000 needed to kick-start the business and open the first Il Giornale store. You can be sure those backers were glad they did. When he acquired Starbucks, he kept the name and rebranded all his own coffee stores as Starbucks. This move instantly increased the number of stores under his control.

Around the turn of the 21st century, Schultz stepped away from the company. When he returned as CEO in 2008, Starbucks was struggling. He helped it recover and soon the company quadrupled in value. In 2014, Starbucks had some 21,000 stores worldwide. Schultz took a business and increased its worth several times over. He's not a one-hit wonder either, having taken a financial stake in a number of other successful businesses such as Groupon and eBay. This billionaire, with a wealth of experience in a variety of roles, is the ideal tutor and advocate for the entrepreneur.

Let's get to learning.

## LEADERSHIP AND INSPIRATION

A strong leader will inspire, and if somebody inspires you, then he or she is most likely a leader. Howard Schultz is inspirational and he is a leader. His philosophy is pretty simple. Schultz believes that you cannot inspire those around you unless you yourself are inspired.

Going way back to the beginning of his involvement with Starbucks, it was easy to see from his philosophy that Schultz was heavily into inspiration.

"We're not in the business of filling bellies; we're in the business of filling souls," he says.

One of the most striking things about Schultz is that while his fame rests largely on Starbucks, it is by no means his greatest passion. He is far more passionate about taking the company or an idea and developing it into something successful, than he is about coffee.

Schultz will always argue that in running Starbucks he is not in the business of selling coffee, but rather, he is in the business of creating a company that treats people—customers and employees—with respect and dignity.

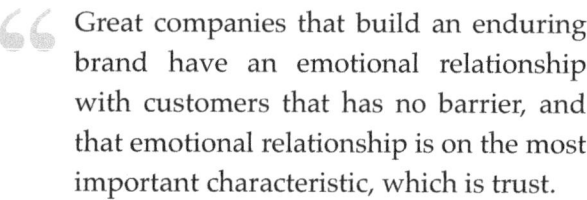

> Great companies that build an enduring brand have an emotional relationship with customers that has no barrier, and that emotional relationship is on the most important characteristic, which is trust.

It's interesting where people pick up their attitudes towards life, leadership, and inspiration. Schultz's father had a menial job. One day he was injured on the job, and he received no compensation for the injury. There was no health insurance and no income for the family. That incident left a lasting impression on Schultz. It is not surprising to see that Starbucks was one of the first companies in America to provide great benefits for its full-time and part-time employees, including comprehensive health insurance and the option to buy company shares.

One of the first inspirational things Schultz did upon returning as CEO in 2008 was to conduct a four-day conference to inspire his 10,000 Starbucks managers. He wanted them to walk away believing in the fact that they, the managers, were personally accountable for everything that happened in their Starbucks stores.

This was not a conference about getting better coffee beans, getting better signage outside of stores, or even offering a wider range of products. This was a conference aimed directly at the way the stores were managed—it was about the attitude of their leaders. By becoming a people person rather than a product person, Schultz was defining the way he led the business, and showing how inspiration was a key component to his leadership style. As Schultz says, "When you're surrounded by people who share a passionate commitment around a common purpose, anything is possible."

## SOCIAL RESPONSIBILITY

Entrepreneurs don't just start businesses and sell products; they also often become community leaders. Schultz's second job title has been 'activist'. While some business leaders refuse to delve into social activism to avoid taking a side and alienating customers, Schultz is the opposite.

> There needs to be a balance between commerce and social responsibility. The companies that are authentic about it will

wind up as the companies that make more money.

In today's business climate, many people are always looking to leave for greener pastures—their current job is only a stepping stone. Schultz's leadership to make Starbucks a great place to work has encouraged loyalty within his team, strengthening the whole operation. The fact that shareholders received an almost 40% return on their shareholdings in recent times is a testament to the fact that Schultz is leading a successful and strong operation.

## IS PROFIT THE MOST IMPORTANT THING?

When Howard Schultz stepped away from Starbucks, profits fell markedly. Starbucks was selling a lot less coffee and the value of their stock was on a steady downward spiral. When Schultz returned to the post of CEO, he turned Starbucks around. How did he do that? How did he get the profits up and the value of the stock to record heights?

Schultz took the attitude that Starbucks was concentrating on sales and not on its message. He believed that if you looked after the people, both employees and customers, then the profits would look after themselves. That attitude and message have proven correct, with Starbucks having recovered and exceeded its earlier success.

It's like the old selling message that you don't sell the actual product, you sell the benefits of having the product. Schultz's attitude was that the Starbucks product would improve the life of the customers in a Starbucks store, as well as the life of the employees who work in those stores.

As an entrepreneur, Schultz has always maintained that he's not interested in the type of business you are in, rather he is interested in what you are passionate about. This is perhaps Schultz's most important lesson.

Do we know what we are actually passionate about? The whole point about Schultz is that his passion, which is deep and rich and widespread, is contagious. People catch his passion, and the consequence of this form of behaviour is that when people catch the passion of the leader, then anything—repeat, anything—is possible.

## SPREADING HIS MESSAGE

Entrepreneurs can influence others more widely by publishing their ideas, as Schultz has. He turned his experiences into two books, in fact. His books *Pour Your Heart Into It: How Starbucks Built a Company One Cup at a Time* and *Onward: How Starbucks Fought for Its Life Without Losing Its Soul* provide insight into his beliefs and attitudes. Both were co-written by other writers. Getting talented people to work with you on various projects enables you to get things done without taking too much of your own time away from your core business.

## STICK TO WHAT YOU KNOW

Entrepreneurs succeed at what they know, and if they don't know, then they hire someone who does. Given his background as a college sports athlete, it is not surprising Schultz used some of his vast wealth to purchase a professional basketball team, the Seattle Supersonics. Alas, dabbling in the NBA did not turn out well. There was controversy between the owner and the some of the players, who felt that Schultz was running the team as a business and not as a sporting club (see the chapter on Alan Sugar later in this book, for a similar case with Tottenham Hotspur). The disagreements between star players and the owner became a public soap opera.

After a few years, Schultz sold the Seattle Supersonics, and the new owner chose to move the team to another state. Naturally, many fans felt upset, blaming Schultz. As a result, his reputation took a hit. Perhaps in an attempt to win back public sentiment, Schultz took legal action against the new owners, claiming that fraud had taken place. Further damaging his reputation, Schultz withdrew the lawsuit. This was a business venture to forget, and Schultz focused again on what he knew: coffee.

## FINAL THOUGHT

Given his success, you might think that Schultz attended the Harvard Business School and was famous for his detailed business plans to create his great wealth. None of that is true. He started work at the lower levels, selling coffee machines. When he broadened his horizons by travelling to Europe and discovering the coffee-shop ambience and its products, he was inspired. What, as entrepreneurs, can we do in our industries to create ideas, inspire thought and open our minds to new possibilities to innovate?

Schultz went it alone and created his own Italian-style coffee shop in America. He persuaded people to invest in his idea. He inspired them. At each step he inspired people, from staff to investors to customers.

Schultz has certainly made mistakes. He freely admits that he has done things that didn't work out, but he continues to persist. Throughout all of his business dealings, the thing that drives him the most has been his belief in being passionate. By all means have a good product and a good business plan, but to be genuinely successful you must be passionate about helping others and aligning that passion with the core of your business.

## 16

## INDRA NOOYI

Indra Nooyi lives in Connecticut, USA. Current net worth: US$144 million.

From India to Pepsi: the rise of Indra Nooyi

You may not know her name, but you definitely know her company's drinks. In 2014, *Fortune* magazine ranked Indra Nooyi the third most powerful woman in business. After five years, as chief financial officer of PepsiCo, she was promoted in 2006 to become only the fifth chief executive officer in Pepsi's 44-year history. A renowned leader, Nooyi admits that, "Leadership is hard to define and good leadership even harder. But if you can get people to follow you to the ends of the earth, you are a great leader." A simple but effective view.

To say that Pepsi has boomed under her watch would be an understatement. Since 2001, when she became the CFO after seven years with Pepsi, the company's annual income rose by more than 70% and net profit more than doubled. In 2011, as the CEO of Pepsi, her salary package topped $17 million.

Born in 1955, Indra Nooyi spent her formative years in her homeland of India. Her early education took place there, and she graduated in 1974 with her first degree in physics, chemistry, and mathematics. She began working in India for Johnson & Johnson as a product manager. In 1978, she was admitted to the Yale School of Management, where she earned a Master's degree. She remained in the United States—she's now a US citizen—and held a number of executive positions at various companies, including Motorola, before starting at Pepsi.

She was responsible for a major restructuring of the company, which saw it divesting itself of some companies and acquiring others. She led the way during the Pepsi merger with the Quaker Oats Co., which brought Gatorade into the Pepsi stable.

She has maintained her connections with the country of her birth, having served as chairwoman of the US-India Business Council. She is heavily involved on the USIBC's board of directors, which is a group of 60 senior executives who represent a wide cross-section of industries in America. Another prestigious award saw her named as the 2009 Chief Executive Officer of the Year. Imagine the competition she must have faced to win that award. She has also received a number of honorary degrees from colleges and universities, and is regularly featured in annual lists of the best CEOs.

As Pepsi CEO, Nooyi makes sure she is visible and

active. She is always out and about talking to business, academia, and political decision-makers. Intelligent and capable, she is frank with her opinions, and her honesty and openness seem to win many fans. We can pick up business ideas from Nooyi because she spreads her messages often in public speeches and announcements.

## DO YOU HAVE A BALANCED OUTLOOK?

Nooyi is critical of today's leaders, believing that too many of them concentrate solely on the short term, and do not have a balance between short-and long-term ambitions and goals. Nooyi believes that it is wrong to focus on short-term quarterly results, living, as it were, from revenue forecast to result. You need to have a balance. Of course, you need to keep your eye on the short-term, but if you don't have a vision for the long-term, then you are restricting the growth.

## OTHER PLAYERS SHOULD BE PARTNERS AND NOT ENEMIES

Do you regard your competitors in the public or private sector as enemies? Nooyi believes that approach is counterproductive. "Stiff-arming them is simply not going to work. We should walk a mile in their shoes," she says. She believes that her business will thrive and continue to grow by treating other players with respect and understanding. By taking a condescending approach to other CEOs and businesses, you do as much harm to yourself as you do to others. Such an approach has consequences for your own mental wellbeing.

 When you assume negative intent, you're angry. If you take away that anger and assume positive intent, you will be amazed. Your emotional quotient goes up because you are no longer almost random in your response.

## THINK GLOBAL, ACT LOCAL

The environmental movement popularised this slogan, and Nooyi supports all of those green principles. Additionally, she believes the slogan can also apply to other aspects of business, and that it's not outdated—it's as relevant today as it has ever been.

She knows the importance of the global market. She is aware of economic and social changes that occur around the world. For example, she knew that recently, in China, people were concerned that children were losing a strong connection with their parents, a connection that had been part of Chinese society for thousands of years. That connection was always reaffirmed at Chinese New Year, when families would strengthen bonds.

Knowing the cultural norms of China, Nooyi commissioned a nine-minute commercial video that featured three of the brand names controlled by Pepsi (note here that she was able to kill three birds with one stone). The commercial promoted the importance of maintaining China's social traditions in today's modern world. This entertaining, informative, and successful video has been viewed hundreds of millions of times in China. It's a perfect example of how you can think global and act local, how you can promote various components of your business at the same time, and how everyone should make it his or her job to know what's going on in society and the world.

## BE FLEXIBLE

According to Nooyi, one of the most important characteristics every CEO or entrepreneur should have is an open mind. If you are set in your ways, particularly if you are unwilling or unable to listen to suggestions or ideas from others, then you are seriously damaging your business. It might be simply because you believe that as the boss you are the holder of all wisdom. That is a fatal error.

The world is constantly changing. In the area of technology and communication alone there seems to be constant change. You need to keep up with the latest developments. You need to be aware of what your competitors are doing. You need to be able to change.

Just as there are people on committees who are reluctant to accept change, so too are there others who have difficulty adapting. You must become flexible. You must operate in a way that encourages others to give advice or make suggestions, and in which you are free of prejudice and are able to consider all proposals on their merit. "To lead in an ever-changing world, leaders must adapt and stay nimble," Nooyi says.

## PEOPLE ARE NOT MACHINES

According to Nooyi, it is vitally important that all managers and entrepreneurs accept the fact that people have feelings. 'People' includes work colleagues, clients, suppliers, and even competitors. One of the best ways to make a business run smoothly and operate profitably is to strengthen ties with fellow humans. As she puts it, "At the end of the day, don't forget you're a person, don't forget you're a mother, don't forget you're a wife, don't forget you're a daughter."

One example Nooyi uses to explain her philosophy in this matter is that she once sat down and wrote a personal letter to the parents of everyone on her top executive team. Nooyi stated in the letter that she thought these people were exceptional human beings and that their parents should be especially proud of their children—all adults, of course. Does that sound like a good idea to you? Do you think the parents discussed those letters with their children? Because the thoughts were sincere and well expressed, they immediately strengthened the bond between Nooyi and her leading workers. If you can find a way to improve relationships and, more importantly, strengthen the connection between you and the people you work with, then you may well be doing the bottom line of your business a power of good.

What Nooyi did by writing to the parents of her

staff members was unusual and unconventional, and the result was that it caused an outpouring of emotion and appreciation from all concerned. Just as bad news can travel fast and widely, so too can good news and positive information, but with a greater impact.

## TAKE NOTHING FOR GRANTED

You have to understand that Nooyi is not your typical American CEO. She is a woman, she wasn't born in America, and she had few, if any, contacts in the business world when she arrived in America. None of which is statistically in her favour.

In many ways, she is a self-made woman. At Pepsi, she was the first woman and first foreign-born person to enter the higher ranks of the company. But nobody gets to be the CEO of a billion-dollar company without having talent. This is both a great achievement and a great responsibility.

Nooyi undertook a detailed and specific tertiary education and worked in a variety of fields with different companies to improve her work expertise and experience. When she joined Pepsi, it took a number of years for her to gain promotion to CEO. Despite this great success, Nooyi always maintains that she will never take anything for granted. "I have an immigrant mentality," she says, "which is that the job can be taken away at any time, so make sure you are in it every day." Is this an attitude that sits well with you? Do you have a born-to-rule mentality or a 'make sure you're in it' mentality?

As an entrepreneur, you may be wondering what

you can do right now to improve your ability as an operator. There are many books you can read (like this one) and videos you can watch, but Nooyi has some interesting recollections of how she got to the top, and more importantly how she is able to continue operating as a top-flight executive with outstanding results. Her experience in consulting positions was vital:

> I don't think I could have gotten here without a strategy-consultant background because it taught me how to think. It taught me how to think of the problem in micro terms but also to zoom out and put the problem in the context of its broader environment and then zoom back in to solve the problem.

Can you get hands-on experience in another's businesses to expand your thinking?

## LEADERSHIP EXPANDS IN DIFFERENT WAYS

Nooyi did not begin as a top-rated executive on day one of her business career. It took her a number of years with steady progress through the ranks. One thing she came to learn throughout her journey was that the more responsibility she was given and the higher she climbed the executive ladder, the greater were her responsibilities.

Once she became a CEO, she found that she had to draw on all of her past business experiences, as well as any skills and abilities she had developed along the way. But more importantly, she had to commit to go on learning, to continuous self-improvement. Nooyi draws a very clear parallel with the situation: "The more the leader is willing to expand and grow, the more vibrant the organisation will be."

There has never been a more specific description of how an entrepreneur can improve his or her business.

> If you want to improve the organisation, you have to improve yourself, and your business gets pulled up with you. That is a big lesson. I cannot just expect the organisation to improve if I don't improve myself and lead the organisation.

So, there you have it. The success of your business, and your success as an entrepreneur depends on your ability to improve, to grow, and to get better. First, you need to know the area or areas in which you need to improve. Second, you need specific steps that you must take to achieve that improvement. But the link is very clear. If you get better, then your business gets better. So, keep reading, because you're already doing it!

## WHAT ARE YOUR SLEEP PATTERNS?

Leading executives disagree on how much sleep one needs to function well in the entrepreneurial environment. Some argue that you need a full eight hours of sleep per day, and one even advocates that you add an extra 30 minutes to that eight hours.

Nooyi doesn't believe in either. She is described as a tireless worker who sleeps only four or five hours a night. She doesn't know how to stop and smell the roses, so to speak. "You must continually increase your learning, the way you think, and the way you approach the business. I have never forgotten that," she says.

Nooyi is also renowned for being a stickler for details and for getting her hands dirty. She is constantly out and about looking to see what is happening with the products of the company. It is not unusual for Nooyi to drop into local retailers to see how Pepsi products are displayed in local stores.

> I notice everything. The printing quality —if the printing is bad or if the colours are off. If it's a Hispanic store and we don't have enough Hispanic offerings there. Why isn't this merchandise available so that the shopper can pick things up easily? I pick up the details that drive the organisation insane. But sweating the details is more important than anything else.

Are you an entrepreneur who spends all of your time locked in your office, with little or no idea of what is actually happening on the floor of your business or in stores where your customers buy your products or services? In the case of one of the leading CEOs in American business, nothing is more important than a face-to-face encounter with the people who purchase or handle the products.

## FINAL THOUGHT

One of few women to achieve such a high rank in business, Nooyi is unique in that regard. In many ways, her philosophies contrast with the ideas of other entrepreneurs described in this book. She's competitive and demanding, but she's also about creating a community with respect and dignity. In the competitive world of business, those principles are sometimes forgotten in the chase for dollars.

If you're looking for down-to-earth advice, then pondering the thoughts of Indra Nooyi could prove invaluable. It won't cost you much, if anything, to put into practice the many things she does. And who knows, it might just make you a happier entrepreneur and help your bottom line move to previously unknown positive places—win-win.

## 17

## WARREN BUFFETT

Warren Buffett lives in Nebraska, USA. Current net worth: US$76.1 billion.

Sage investment advice from icon Warren Buffett

Star investor Warren Buffett *can* predict the future. He once said boldly, "I always knew I was going to be rich. I don't think I ever doubted it for a minute." He was right. Born in 1930, he's now one of the richest men in the world thanks to his savvy investing skills through his holding corporation, Berkshire Hathaway. Berkshire Hathaway has nearly US$200 billion in revenue each year, and Buffett's net worth is over US$70 billion.

Buffett had some advantages in his upbringing. His father was a congressman in the United States and ran a brokerage firm. Nonetheless, as a teenager he learned the importance of working and saving his income. In high school, he was already an entrepreneur. He sold golf balls and washed cars, worked in his grandfather's local store, and even sold chewing gum and magazines door-to-door.

When he was only 10 years old, he was taken on a trip to New York City, and one of the tourist attractions for young Warren was to see the New York Stock Exchange. At age 14, he completed a tax return and claimed a deduction for the use of a bicycle when working on his local paper route. At the end of his high school days, Buffett received a report from a teacher that said, "He likes mathematics and would make a good stockbroker." You could almost say he was born to invest.

Today, he is quite frugal in his spending, living in the same house he bought in 1958. He maintains the same basic salary of US$100,000 a year, and that hasn't changed for the last 25 years. A few years ago, Bill Gates convinced Buffett to donate the vast majority of his wealth to charitable causes through the Bill & Melinda Gates Foundation.

Let's now look at some specific advice on entrepreneurial success from Buffett.

## THREE BASICS OF INVESTMENT

The main lessons he learned in college are the lessons he has followed all his life. He believes the three basics of investment never change. Those basics are as follows:

- Stocks and shares should be regarded as a business

- You need to use the market fluctuation to benefit your cause
- You should always seek a margin of safety.

Despite his personal prediction above, Buffett says we can't predict the future. More than half a century ago he predicted that stock prices would in some cases be up 20%, in some cases would be down 20%, and the rest would be somewhere in between. In other words, you take a risk when you invest money and time in stocks or in business, and you need to be in the business for the long haul. "Our favourite holding period is forever," he says.

Of course, you want to be wary of losing everything, but it's important that you understand the ebb and flow of the stock market in the world of business. Before you start to operate as an investor or as an entrepreneur, understand the fact that good and bad times are part and parcel of everyday life.

One trick Buffett uses is that when a particular idea or project is likely to happen, he lists all the possibilities of failure. He asks how it could go wrong. Then, looking at those points, he either makes a decision to abandon the project, or he takes action to cover his losses should the worst happen.

Could you look at opportunities and problems with the same process as Buffett?

## TWO INGREDIENTS

The two main ingredients Buffett talks about when it comes to investment are 1) homework and 2) patience.

Without these two factors, so much of your success is down to luck. Buffett says that there's no guarantee, of course, but by spending a great deal of time doing sensible research, you are doing your homework. And being prepared to wait for the right price or, as an entrepreneur, for the right time, you seriously improve your chances of being successful. It's a tortoise and hare situation. Being the tortoise has a lot of advantage, Buffett believes.

Don't follow the masses. Some people would suggest that if an area is hot then you should jump aboard the bandwagon. Buffett's philosophy is that if everybody else is doing it, that's an excellent reason to avoid it.

Never stop learning. Buffett's philosophy is that you should go to bed a little wiser than when you woke up. Make every day a winning day. If you have only one goal in life, make it this one. Improve every day. Learn something every day. Buffett believes that if you follow this maxim you will never run out of ideas and never run out of customers to serve.

## KNOW THE MOOD SWINGS OF THE ECONOMY

Understanding the cycles of business and, in Buffett's case, understanding the cycles in investing goes a long way and accomplishes two things. It helps you keep your sanity and it helps you understand the way to be successful. Buffett quickly understood that your chances of thriving greatly improved when the market was in your favour and that the opposite would occur when the market wasn't in your favour. Just the fact that he understood this principle enabled him to take the long-term view. How can this apply to you as an entrepreneur?

First, you need to think macro (big picture) as well as micro (small picture) when it comes to your business. You have to continually contextualise the workings of your business and decisions relating to it. This means putting them in context of the environment in which you and your business operate.

Secondly, it's important that you understand the ebb and flow of the business cycle and be prepared to be very successful at sometimes and to be less successful or even struggle at other times. Knowing that this cycle occurs enables you to handle the tough times when they come. Rather than stress out and suffer enormously when things are going badly, you'll be prepared for this situation. You'll be able to ride out the storm.

 Look at market fluctuations as your friend rather than your enemy, and profit from folly rather than participate in it.

## WHAT RULES SHOULD WE SET FOR OURSELVES?

As an entrepreneur how should we judge ourselves? Is it as simple as a basic profit and loss statement? Well, obviously yes, in terms of surviving; but Buffett takes a different approach. He doesn't declare the year to be successful depending on whether or not these stocks may show a profit. He judges his performance in comparison to that of the Dow Index. So, long as his results were better than the national yardstick, even if he made a loss, he regards that year as being successful.

## TREAT YOUR PARTNERS WITH RESPECT

It has long been a practice in the world of buying and selling stocks that investors rarely, if ever, get to know the person in charge of their money. How does that person think or make decisions? Buffett was an exception. He was prepared to treat his partners as equals. Translating that into the world of the entrepreneur, Buffett teaches us about the importance of working closely with anyone who has invested in your business. Be open and frank with them. Treat them not just as a partner but also as an equal.

Buffett is very much his own man. He has very strong principles, and he is not swayed by public opinion. This could very well apply to you as an entrepreneur. Know who you are and be confident in that knowledge. Buffett had some interesting ideas way back 1962, but they hold true today.

> You will not be right simply because a large number of people momentarily agree with you. You will not be right simply because important people agree with you. You will be right over the course of many transactions, if your hypotheses are correct, your facts are correct, and your reasoning is correct.

## THE IMPORTANCE OF REPUTATION

Buffett quite openly says that he will not trade reputation for money. Losing money is never a satisfactory experience, but it is something from which you can recover. Losing your reputation is worse. Your reputation is far more important than anything else. By all means seek to be as successful as possible, but never jeopardise your reputation. "It takes 20 years to build a reputation and five minutes to ruin it. If you think about that, you'll do things differently," he says.

Buffett's opinion on reputation is even more relevant in the Digital Age. You need to be careful about what you say and do because today the whole world is watching. Protect your brand.

## THE COURAGE TO DEAL WITH FAILURE

Nobody wants to fail, but sometimes you only learn to succeed once you've had some failure in your life. Courage is not something that you can buy in a shop. You develop courage when you are faced with hardship and you work your way through. The real entrepreneur is somebody who makes it outside of his or her comfort zone. It's easy to be successful and to make money when everything is going your way. What really counts is being successful and not quitting when life is tough.

When starting and operating a business, every entrepreneur runs the risk of failure. Having courage is simply having faith, faith to leap when at times you don't know what you'll land on. Buffett has a simple philosophy in this regard and says that risk comes from not knowing what you're doing. His idea is to go slow on the huge projects until you have the risk factors under control.

## FINAL THOUGHT

Warren Buffett is undoubtedly a magician when it comes to investment and making money. The Oracle of Omaha's almost homespun philosophy is what has worked for him for decades.

Buffett sets realistic goals. He avoids expectations that are doomed to failure. He spends an inordinate amount of time on homework or in preparing a case before he invests in a particular project. He looks at all the possibilities of failure and then develops a risk strategy that will enable him to keep going and survive should some of the failure possibilities come true.

Like most great entrepreneurs, he is anything but a selfish person. Where he can donate his time and money to worthwhile causes, he does so. The world is a better place now because of Buffett's investing acumen and, as entrepreneurs, we can all learn from his long-term success.

## 18

## SARA BLAKELY

Sara Blakely lives in Atlanta, Georgia, USA. Current net worth: US$1.06 billion.

### Starting from the bottom: Sara Blakely and women's undergarments

Like many women at some stage in their lives, Sara Blakely found herself frustrated by clothing options. "I had these white pants that I had spent a lot of money on, and you get home and you think, 'What am I really supposed to wear under this?'" she says. In what she calls a "frustrated consumer moment" she came up with the idea for Spanx, a line of female undergarments that she has turned into a multi-million-dollar company, and that has made her one of the youngest self-made billionaires.

The journey to create Spanx was a difficult one, with roadblocks at every stage. She knew what she wanted to design—an undergarment that would smooth out women's 'saddlebags' and 'muffin tops', as she called them, without being noticeable—and she knew that a patent would be required. Since she couldn't find a single female patent lawyer, she bought a book on patent writing and wrote a patent herself. Blakely had been told that it was easier to get a patent if you had a word that was not spelled the conventional way, and while driving in her car she thought of the name Spanx for her 'shapewear'.

With Sara as the model, Blakely's artist mother drew an example of her daughter's undergarment design. Blakely took a week off work and drove around the state of North Carolina, where many of America's hosiery mills were located. All the mills were owned and operated by men, the majority of them unhelpful.

She was ready to give up when one of the mill managers contacted her and said he had had second thoughts. Why? He had two daughters, and when he explained Blakely's idea to them, they said it was brilliant.

That was really just the start. It took a long time to find the perfect design and almost as long to get shops and stores to stock her items. She had no money for advertising and would often simply stand at a meeting-fair stall and talk to women. Her big break came when she sent a collection of her undergarments to Oprah Winfrey, who gave them a ringing endorsement.

Born in 1971, Blakely went to college and did a

degree in communications, thinking she would become a lawyer. She studied the entrance exam, but failed, and changed her career direction. She went to work for the Disney Corporation for a few months and then became a door-to-door salesperson, selling fax machines. By night she was a stand-up comic (a tough gig!). Then came Spanx.

Let's now look at what made this entrepreneur so successful despite her unusual path to creating her company.

### FAILURE IS NEVER JUST FAILURE

Apparently, Blakely's father gave wise advice to all of his children, and at the end of each day he would ask, "So what did you fail at today?" If his children said that they hadn't failed at anything that day, he would be disappointed. There was a definite method in his madness. He wanted his children to understand that failure came about through a lack of trying, through not taking yourself out of your comfort zone and not trying to achieve something that you've never achieved before. The bigger the failure then the better the lesson.

Those lessons that Sara and her siblings learned in their childhood certainly paid enormous dividends when, as a young woman, she hit on the idea for Spanx.

 I think failure is nothing more than life's way of nudging you that you are off-course. My attitude to failure is not attached to outcome, but in not trying. It is liberating. Most people attach failure to something not working out, or how people perceive you. This way, it is about answering to yourself.

## DO YOU HAVE THE IMAGINATION?

Blakely says she could imagine her success long before it happened. She talks about the fact that she could see herself performing on the Oprah Winfrey TV show some 15 years before it actually happened. By having this imagination, by having this vision of what could be, she was able to create goals and find the motivation to keep going to achieve those goals. Are you able to see into the future and imagine a clear picture of what your business could be and could do? Do you have a vision?

## GET THE FOUNDATION RIGHT FIRST

Blakely had an idea for an undergarment that had none of the old and disappointing aspects of pantyhose, but she didn't tell family and friends straight away. She says that she spent about a year working on the ideal prototype. The reasoning behind this thinking is that if you tell people your idea too soon, before you've got all the problems sorted out, people will criticise you. If you've done all of your homework first, and only talk about your idea when you are rock-

solid in your belief, you will be ready to kno
cism back. Are you jumping the gun on an id
you've really brainstormed it?

## DON'T GIVE UP

Every person, from experts to friends and family will preach this, but when you study the life of Blakely you suddenly realise just how relevant and important it is.

People asked her a number of questions. Who are you? Which company do you represent? Who are your backers? To each of these questions Sara provided the same answer: her name. Every door was slammed in her face. "My training of cold-calling and everyone under the sun telling me 'no', and my keeping going, was a huge part of the first two years of Spanx." How easy would it have been for her to give up? But because she didn't give up, her luck turned.

She got a patent, she got a working model, and she then had to promote the product, get backers, and get people to buy the product. She had no money for advertising, so did it all with her own effort.

Are you practising getting told 'no' enough, and keeping your stride? How do you deal with rejection?

## HIRING THE RIGHT PEOPLE

This is always a tricky subject. Blakely went out on a limb and hired people inexperienced in her product area to run her product development and public relations. So, what did they have going for them? Two things: they were friends of Sara Blakely, and they believed in her product and supported her right from the beginning. Despite the risk, the people succeeded. Do you hire skill or do you hire will? What value do you place on a person with absolute belief in your vision and offering?

## YOU CAN WING IT

Blakely began receiving requests for media coverage before she even had a detailed marketing plan in place. Rather than panic and give up, she simply got stuck in and figured it out as she went along—she was able to wing it. "You've got to embrace what you don't know," she says.

At one stage, the Oprah Winfrey show wanted to film Blakely and her staff meeting in their offices. The only problem was that she didn't have any staff and she didn't have any offices! She quickly called a bunch of her friends, and even the parcel-post employee who was helping send her Spanx, and asked them to pretend they worked for her. They all dropped what they were doing and ran to Blakely's apartment to support her. Needless to say, she was able to think on her feet. "Oprah had chosen Spanx as one of her favourite products in 2000," she says. "I had boxes of product in my apartment and I had two weeks' notice that she was going to say she loved it on TV, and I had no shipping department." Blakely got that product out though—that's improvisation!

Are you stuck in 'analysis paralysis', over-thinking everything when maybe a leap of faith is in order?

## STUDY ON THE JOB

A lot of success as an entrepreneur can come from experimenting, making mistakes, and learning on the job. Sara Blakely is an ideal example of this. She wasn't a trained designer of women's undergarments. She had no experience at all in the manufacturing and marketing worlds. She didn't know anything about IT and website development. She'd never set up a website or operated an online store.

What she did have was an idea and a passion to make that idea a reality. The point here is that if you have the idea and you have the commitment and the energy to work at that idea until it succeeds, that is all you need. If you're missing skills or strategies you then need to go out and get them.

## FORGET THE TRAPPINGS TO START WITH

So many entrepreneurs think that it's important to lease a car, lease an office space, and set up a huge website with all the bells and whistles. That, in fact, can be a serious handicap to the success of an entrepreneur.

Sara Blakely started work in her apartment. She didn't lease a vehicle or lease an office. She didn't even have a proper website. She covered all the bases first while operating with minimum overheads. Only when she had covered all the bases and was ready to go did she start looking at an office. The key is to make sure your idea is sound and that you've investigated all the possibilities of making it successful first. Don't spend your money until you are ready to launch your product, and more importantly, don't waste it on luxuries (yes, like an office and a desk!). Spend it on marketing, innovation and delivering your brand promise.

## JUST BECAUSE THEY DO IT THAT WAY DOESN'T MAKE IT RIGHT

So, you have an idea and you go out into the real world to test your idea. You constantly get knocked back. Perhaps it's not your idea that's at fault, but the system. When Blakely first decided to go with her idea about improving female undergarments, she couldn't believe the information she discovered.

There was a ridiculous sizing protocol that was used in the manufacture of every product, where garments had only one average waist measurement regardless of the size of the garment. How crazy was that? Also, any new products were tested on mannequins and never on models. Could it be that the female undergarment industry was dominated by males who didn't understand female undergarments? It took a woman to see the stupidity of the system. Don't assume the structure and the ways and means of doing things to be correct.

Disruption is the new black—billionaires in the 21st century, especially in the tech industry, are challenging the norm and looking at problems to solve, not just making the same thing as everyone else.

Are you disrupting your industry?

**FINAL THOUGHT**

Sara Blakely is the ideal poster person for any budding entrepreneur. She literally let nothing stand in her way. She was also very smart in her approach. She knew that the best people to give advice to her about female undergarments were females who wore undergarments. Looking for marketing inspiration, she would show the packaging she was thinking of using to a number of females. Her mother was a great source of inspiration as well.

When she came up with the tag line 'Don't worry, we've got your butt covered!' and heard the natural laughter from the women about it, she knew she had a hit on her hands.

She was also a great believer in her own product. How important is that in your role as an entrepreneur? Here is a perfect example. She rang the buyer of a major department store that was based in another state. Blakely described her product and said she would like to demonstrate it for the buyer. The woman agreed. Blakely took a plane to the woman and the store, and she physically demonstrated the difference her undergarment made to her body shape. She won a huge order from this prestigious store. Now that's what you call believing in your own product.

She also worked hard on her marketing and once her product was available in a particular store, she would call her friends and ask them to go into the store and make a fuss about her products. She was even prepared to pay her friends to buy her own products. This may seem a little weird to some, but it was brilliant and it absolutely worked. Blakely was a go-getter who made a killing through a great idea and outstanding determination. She didn't just follow a path given to her, her default path; she quite literally designed her own way.

# 19

## ALAN SUGAR

Alan Sugar lives in Essex, UK. Current net worth: US$2.17 billion.

### The bittersweet career of Alan Sugar

Billionaire English businessman and *The Apprentice* TV star Alan Sugar once said, "You can't learn business expertise from a book." But don't let that stop you; keep reading, because the story of Sugar's rise to the top includes valuable entrepreneurial lessons from a man who started with nothing. Born to Jewish parents in London in 1947, Sugar is now one of the wealthiest men in Britain, with a pilot's licence and a taste for classic cars, particularly of the Rolls Royce variety.

Having been knighted Sir Alan, and more recently having been elevated to the House of Lords, he can now be addressed as Baron Sugar. Baron Sugar has written an autobiography titled *What You See Is What You Get*, and that's a pretty good description of the man. Whatever else Sugar is, you could never call him a shrinking violet—he's definitely not soft-spoken. He is famous, or perhaps infamous, for speaking his mind, and then some. With that warning out of the way, here are some of Sugar's business tips from a lifetime of experience.

## STARTING YOUR BUSINESS VENTURE

Despite his own challenges, Sugar speaks critically of entrepreneurs who develop a chip on their shoulder about their failure to raise financing for their next ventures. "I am sick and tired of this free-lunch culture and of people asking, 'Where can I get some money?' It's the disease that caused banks to collapse," Sugar says.

Some entrepreneurs think that investors, or their family, or society in general owes them something. According to Sugar, this is absolutely incorrect thinking. If you genuinely want to succeed, you need to create your own opportunities. It's the Fred Astaire philosophy of the harder you work, the luckier you become.

This attitude likely developed from Sugar's humble upbringing. His father was a tailor in the rag trade in the East End of London, and young Alan lived in a council flat with his family. He went to government schools and did not attend university. Leaving school at age 16, he briefly became a civil or public servant before he went into business for himself. To say that he is a self-made man would be an understatement—he had only £50 to his name when he started.

Sugar describes the difficult but influential circumstances of his upbringing.

> I grew up in the 1950s when times were really tough. My father didn't know whether he had any work the next day. Government handouts were far fewer, and far more difficult to obtain. You had to fend for yourself. The only way to get ahead was to work hard. Even when I was going to school I had part-time jobs.

## PREPARATION

Considering his formative experiences in London, Sugar believes the best way to receive entrepreneurial funding is to work hard and prepare thoroughly. Sugar thinks that having connections with important people, going on business lunches, and trying to get yourself into the good books of investors and institutions are not the best ways to achieve success. Sugar believes that you should stop dreaming that some magical person is going to suddenly step forward with a vast sum of money just for your project. Instead, do your homework and produce detailed, easy-to-understand plans and financials.

Sugar certainly has a history of major business success to back up his advice. His electronics company Amstrad—named using a short form of Alan Michael

Sugar Trading—did exceptionally well with a number of products. One of his secrets is to make a business as risk-free or as safe as possible. If you have an extremely risky situation, then first of all you will have difficulty attracting finance. Secondly, when you do get financing, the rate of return demanded by the lender will be much greater. If you can decrease the level of risk in your venture two things will happen: you will be more attractive to a greater number and variety of lenders; and they will be less inclined to charge a higher rate because they are more confident that you have a lower risk enterprise.

Note that he says you should lower risk, not eliminate it. In reality, business risk can't be completely eliminated. Sugar's life exemplifies this truism. Produced through Amstrad, his range of personal computers gained a bad reputation because of unreliable hard disks. Seagate produced these hard disks, and Sugar was not averse to seeking legal action when he felt his business interests were compromised. Sugar sued Seagate and won an out-of-court settlement of US$22 million. Call it a learning experience. As the saying goes, the customer is always right (almost always, that is), and any cutting of corners or sloppiness on your behalf is the ideal way for the customer to become dissatisfied. By being totally committed to your business, you minimise the possibility that the customer will complain.

Sugar also faced risk in the realm of the football business—in which he didn't have experience—after taking over as the owner of London-based soccer club Tottenham Hotspur in 1991. Just as he did on his television show *The Apprentice*, where he fires one of the contestants every program until only one remains, Sugar hired and fired managers at Tottenham on a regular basis—even the well-liked Terry Venables. He sacked Venables on the eve of the FA Cup final. When he sold his ownership of the football club in 2001, his parting words were that his time at Tottenham was "a waste of my life".

As was the case at Tottenham, it's pointless to keep pumping money into a venture that is just not working. Sugar has learned that you should only take risks on things that you understand, and that you should stick to what you know. If you are not an expert in any aspect of your business, then employ a mentor who is. If your talents are better spent elsewhere in the business, then so be it—get another expert to take on tasks that you can't or won't do. If you give yourself the freedom to concentrate on your area of expertise, then you give the business a much greater chance of success.

In this way, Sugar believes that you should make the most of the assets and talent you have. You might be lucky and raise additional funds, but it is most important that you do not overstretch yourself financially, particularly when it comes to marketing. Do what you do best and do it to the best of your ability. If you set mini-goals and achieve them, then you show yourself to be a successful entrepreneur and will be far more attractive to would-be investors.

## LEARNING ON THE JOB

Of course it would be wonderful if your business was an overnight success, but the fact is that very few are. You need to have the right idea, business model, people, funding and timing, and all of that can take time and can involve trial and error. It's fine to expect success, but don't set your short-term expectations too high. If you do, it is so much easier to become disappointed from the outset; you need to build your success step by step.

Sugar looks to his failures as positives:

> If you want to be a successful entrepreneur, you have to get in and make mistakes and learn from them. Studying business is a worthwhile activity, but it's important to understand that the way to become an entrepreneur is to get your hands dirty. Nobody teaches you how to turn an idea into reality or how to know when a good deal is a good deal. You learn these things by doing things.

When Sugar is looking for employees, he chooses those who have hands-on experience.

> Qualifications are certainly important, but all such pieces of paper are not the only thing. What really appeals to me is the experience a person has had in the

> workplace. I've always said that if you want to own and operate an airline the first thing you should do is become a baggage handler, and then someone who works on the desk in the airport, and then perhaps move on to becoming a manager. It's only when you understand the various tasks that are required in the business that you are really able to act as a top-level manager or CEO. As far as work experience is concerned, never shirk a job.

Sugar believes that this on-the-job experience is important for two good reasons. Firstly, it keeps your mind active and keeps you on your toes. Secondly, the world—certainly the world of technology—is constantly changing, meaning you simply have to learn new skills to keep up.

## EFFECTIVE HABITS

The link between a hardworking spirit and business success may seem obvious to the likes of Sugar. But for many, it can be easy to fall into bad habits during the working day. If you are late to work or spend far too much time socialising or having long lunches, or not getting enough sleep and eating poorly, you not only run the risk of damaging your health, but also allow your competitor a distinct advantage.

Sugar believes that to be successful as an entrepreneur your desire for success has to come from within. You can't pretend to be ambitious and you can't fake a desire to be successful. One of the ways you can make contact with your inner self is to find a role model or a mentor like the many in this book— who you admire greatly. Study their beliefs and their actions, because they are the things that create the results and form your habits, both good and bad.

Every entrepreneur will go through difficult times like the ones Sugar has faced. Some of those times involve periods where you have been trying exceptionally hard, taking care of yourself, working long hours, and doing everything possible to make your business a success. When the tough times come, the only thing that matters is your perseverance. You should never blindly carry on, but carry on thinking about what is happening and how you can work your way through the problem. If you believe that your idea and your plan are on track, then never give up.

You need to be absolutely crystal-clear on your goal. To have a vision of what you want to achieve and where you want to finish up, you need to use your imagination. You need to make sure you're using your brain to its full capacity. You need to think outside the box (and then outside that!). Sugar believes that you can train your brain to concentrate on doing only the tasks required for achievement.

## FINAL THOUGHT

Alan Sugar has made too many business mistakes to list. Electronic products failed, Tottenham Hotspur floundered for years, and he remarked in 2005 that the iPad wouldn't last 12 months.

Just as he has made mistakes, he has also had some brilliant successes. The fact that he's a guru for young entrepreneurs—he has even started *The Apprentice* in a new format for teenage entrepreneurs—shows how widely he is respected. He is a well-known benefactor of many worthy causes, and at least two British universities have awarded him honorary degrees.

His outrageous personality obviously helps, but if you cut through the bravado you will find a man who speaks his mind from experience. He knows what it's like to boil beetroots in a bath before he sets off for school in the morning. He's done all of the boring and mundane jobs, and he knows the business of business. People listen to Alan Sugar because he's been successful and has plenty of practical and beneficial advice.

From Sugar's successes and failures, you can learn to set achievable goals. Do your homework, don't believe the world owes you a living, and be prepared if necessary to cut your losses. Behind every great successful entrepreneur is a man or woman who makes mistakes, learns from them, and keeps on keeping on. And finally, it is Sugar's hard work and laser focus that have seen him get it done over his career, attributes that a lot of entrepreneurs need to pay attention to.

# 20

## LARRY ELLISON

Larry Ellison lives in California. Current net worth: US$51.9 billion.

Larry Ellison, the Oracle of entrepreneurship

Brash, outspoken, and exceedingly successful, Larry Ellison leads a movie-star life that is a product of his entrepreneurship. Started with seed funding of only US$2000, his company Oracle now leads in the area of data storage and information sharing.

Oracle and its boss are associated with other things too, such as the BMW Oracle yacht-racing team. Ellison has been heavily involved in arguably the most prestigious yachting race, the Louis Vuitton Cup. He even owns his own island—yes, an island. Divorced four times, Ellison once said, "Who am I winning for? Am I winning for Oracle shareholders or is it simply a matter of personal vanity? I'll admit to it. Mea culpa. An awful lot of it is personal vanity."

Ellison didn't, however, start with a silver spoon in his mouth. Born in New York in 1944 to an unmarried mother, he caught pneumonia as a baby, and his mother gave him away to her aunt and uncle. He didn't see her again for almost 50 years.

Ellison attended college in Chicago, dropping out twice before moving to California and working in a variety of jobs, often associated with computers. Now, semi-retired and one of the wealthiest men in the world, his fortune, listed at approximately US$49.3 billion, includes an impressive portfolio of real estate, with a residence in California valued at over US$100 million.

Ellison has created an image that stands out. He dates supermodels and he travels at breakneck speeds on land and sea and in the air. A daredevil in mountain biking and body surfing, he often suffers injuries, some of them serious. He's rarely out of the news, whether for his personal life or his business battles.

It's hard to tell if Larry Ellison is the type of person he is because of the money he has created, or whether he was always that sort of person. Perhaps his innate personality is what led to his success. Let's look at some of the principles that made Ellison successful.

## THE ROLE OF SELF-EDUCATION

You don't have to complete college or university to be a successful entrepreneur. Like many of the entrepreneurs who made a fortune in Silicon Valley, Larry Ellison fits a certain mould: he was a college dropout who made it big. Like Bill Gates, Michael Dell and Ellison's close friend, the late Steve Jobs, higher education wasn't a key to his success.

How good are we at learning? Where can we learn —at school or on the job? We can go to college or university and we can certainly take courses, but how quick are we on the uptake outside of the classroom? Outside of school, Ellison created the database that became Oracle after simply reading a document about databases written by an IBM scientist. As an entrepreneur, do you have the ability to self-educate as Ellison did? (Reading this book is a great start!)

When you use a credit card or purchase a prescription drug from your pharmacist, the information is probably transferred to an Oracle database. Ellison created the building blocks of e-commerce, and says, "Our goal is very simply to become the desktop for e-businesses."

**COMPETITION, GREED, AND AGGRESSION**

The greatest sports people in the world all have one thing in common: they are driven to win. As a yachtsman, Larry Ellison is fiercely competitive. He looks at all manner of changes he can make to his yachts to make them go faster. He studies the tactics and techniques of sailing to be a better yachtsman. It is this same attitude that he took to business and to his company Oracle.

If you were to ask Ellison why he remained so passionate about his work for so long, he would tell you that it is because he loves to compete. He knows it is not easy to be successful, and he knows that he has to continue to evolve to progress and to remain competitive. "I'm addicted to winning. The more you win, the more you want to win," Ellison says.

While some may think that greed is not a positive, Ellison is proud of the fact that he earns a whopping annual salary of close to $100 million. He believes that executives who do wonderful things for companies and their shareholders should be handsomely rewarded. Are you underselling yourself? If you have achieved great success, and particularly if you have been the creator or co-creator of your business, then why should you not be adequately rewarded? Are you underselling your worth and receiving a salary that is not commensurate with your expertise and experience?

Ellison's salary is a product of his aggression in what is a competitive business. Before he came along, CEOs in the corporate world rarely, if ever, publicly attacked their competitors. Ellison not only attacked his competitors, he did so with relish, such as when he battled with SAP. "When SAP, and specifically Hasso Plattner, said they're going to build this in-memory database and compete with Oracle, I said, 'God, get me the name of that pharmacist, they must be on drugs'," Ellison says.

In this battle, he ran huge ads not only boasting about the improved performance of Oracle, but also pointing out the lousy results of its competitors. Before Ellison, this type of public criticism was fairly unheard of. How aggressive should you be in promoting your business?

## SPEND YOUR MONEY WISELY

While Ellison spends his money on extravagant things —he recently spent US$500 million on a 98% ownership share in a Hawaiian island called Lanai—he can never be accused of frittering away his wealth. He has spent money on real estate, yachts, airplanes, boats, cars and art, and the value of many of these items will appreciate over time. He has made wise investments. While his fabulous wealth is not at risk of disappearing, investing wisely and diversely in things that appreciate in value is a good lesson.

It can also be doubly beneficial for all concerned if, as an entrepreneur, you invest your money in something that can hopefully benefit humankind. Ellison plans to create a program for sustainable farming on Lanai. The lessons he and others working on this project learn could be of valuable assistance to farming communities around the world.

## DO YOU HAVE TO REINVENT YOURSELF?

Every entrepreneur faces this challenge. Do I keep on doing the same thing I've been doing, trying to do it better? Or do I look to expand? If I do expand, do I expand in my own area of expertise or move into a new area? Ellison has no doubts about the answers to these questions. He once mentioned a line about relationships from actor and director Woody Allen. "A relationship is like a shark, it either has to move forward or it dies. And that's true about your company."

Oracle became the world's biggest operator in the database-software business, but that wasn't enough for Ellison. He mounted a controversial takeover of the business-software company PeopleSoft, spending more than US$10 billion on this purchase. Then, Oracle moved into hardware and purchased Sun Microsystems. Where do you stand on the issue of takeovers? Do you have plans to expand and, if so, in which direction? Could you buy a competitor or a complimentary business?

## DO YOU HAVE A LEGACY TO LEAVE?

When you train your staff extremely well, there is sometimes the risk that they will leave you and create their own successful business. Larry Ellison takes pride in the success of one of his former employees, Marc Benioff.

For thirteen years, Benioff was in charge of sales and marketing at Oracle. He was handsomely paid for his work and was very good at what he did—just look at the progress made by Oracle in that time. After some time, Benioff set out on his own and formed a company called Salesforce.com.

Salesforce.com was an unusual business, hiring or renting out computer software as opposed to selling it permanently to the customer. When the company first started, it really struggled. Benioff, like his former boss, stuck at it. Companies like Adobe have recently copied the rental model to avoid the problem of software piracy. Today, businesses are chasing him for what he offers. His net wealth is said to be around $3 billion.

How much kudos should Ellison take from the success of his former marketing boss, someone who has clearly made it on his own? Are you developing and encouraging your staff members to do great things for you?

## HOW TO BE A GOOD CORPORATE CITIZEN

While success may breed an ego and a showy lifestyle, many entrepreneurs like Ellison give back to the community. Many billionaires have publicly announced that they donate vast amounts of money to worthwhile causes and help out their own employees. Bill Gates and Warren Buffett are prime examples of this form of behaviour, leading the way on donations to health-related causes.

Many gurus advocate this behaviour for a number of reasons. It certainly creates good publicity for you and your business. It genuinely assists people less fortunate than you and your fellow workers. Ellison says, "Taking care of your employees is extremely important and very, very visible." It stamps you as a good corporate citizen, and many people would like to get to know and do business with you because of this attitude of giving. Ellison also has made donations to create art museums, a personal interest of his.

Ellison has joined other billionaires in what has become known as The Giving Pledge. This is a project started by Bill Gates and Warren Buffett that encourages billionaires to donate their wealth to worthy causes. Furthermore, Ellison recently had an accident and severely damaged his arm. As a result, he needed microsurgery. He was so impressed with the surgeon that he donated US$5 million to begin a specialist clinic treating similar injuries.

But all of this begs the question: how public should you make your generosity? There are some who believe that donating to charity is an exceptionally good idea but that it should be done privately and without fanfare. That is for you to decide. Ellison takes the approach that he is happy to help others less fortunate, but he doesn't want to make a song and dance about the fact.

## WHEN SHOULD YOU RETIRE?

Many companies ask their CEOs to step down at a certain age. Today IBM requires their CEOs to retire at 60. Ellison is almost 72 and is only now stepping aside from this role, and he will still keep his hand in the business as a board member. The point for entrepreneurs today is that applying restrictions to what you can and can't do can be counterproductive. Do you want to keep working? Are you enthusiastic and passionate about your business? Then don't assume you have to retire at a certain age. I've met and trained many people well into their 80s who are still wanting to learn and grow their business, and are not that excited by golfing for eight hours a day!

## FINAL THOUGHT

We need to separate the headline-making lifestyle of Ellison from the down-to-earth, hard-working genius that grabbed an idea and ran with it. Sure, he plays tough, but life is tough and Ellison is a survivor. While some people may find his public personality and his lavish spending a turn off, Ellison is the sort of entrepreneur with so many qualities and characteristics that you can pick and choose what you like about him and his work, and settle on emulating just those aspects. If you achieve even a fraction of his success, then you will have done very well.

Larry Ellison made it to the top despite a rough start that included an early illness and adoption. He went to college twice and dropped out both times. Traditional education, while hugely helpful to some, didn't play a part in Ellison's success. What Ellison was good at was self-teaching—his success also came from personal initiative. How many books do you read? How many events do you attend? How many courses do you buy, or mentors do you have? Never stop learning.

# 21

## EVAN SPIEGEL

Evan Spiegel lives in California. Current net worth: US$4 billion.

Evan Spiegel, the man who turned down three billion big ones

Maybe it's just a product of the naïve confidence of youth, but 24-year-old Evan Spiegel turned down a buyout offer of US$3 billion dollars. Born in Los Angeles, Spiegel is an entrepreneur with a net worth of about US$4 billion. Being so young, Spiegel doesn't have the track record of many other well-known entrepreneurs, several of whom are old enough to be his grandfather. Nonetheless, his claim to almost instant fame was in creating a highly unusual application called Snapchat.

Snapchat is an app for sending photos, videos, drawings and text, called 'snaps', to a selected group of recipients. On first glance, this sounds wholly unoriginal—so many apps and websites have such features. Indeed, basic email service has allowed such functionality since its invention.

Spiegel also knew all about Facebook, with its multimedia capabilities. It has many great points and is understandably popular, but the website also has what some describe as a fatal flaw: what you post on Facebook stays on Facebook. Millions of people who post something on Facebook regret having done so shortly after.

What's different about Snapchat? Well, Spiegel added a feature that made the app unique: once the recipient views the snaps, they disappear in a few seconds. After that, they are permanently gone from the recipient's device.

As a result, the app has appealed to millions of users in the 18-to-25-year-old bracket, and recent reports state that use in the over 40s market is also growing. Seven hundred million snaps are sent every day, along with 500 million text messages. That's a lot of business. Spiegel took a common idea and added a twist—that's the sign of a sharp mind looking for a new angle.

Some entrepreneurs who develop a successful app or website—Mark Zuckerberg and Facebook is a prime example—face lawsuits from so-called partners who claim part-ownership. This is the same with Spiegel: Spiegel was sued by a fellow student at his university who claimed that he too had contributed ideas to what became a very successful application.

The origins of Snapchat are clearly disputed. One story goes that in the spring of 2011 Spiegel telephoned his fraternity brother Bobby Murphy and told him he had an idea about disappearing pictures and messages. Another version is that Reggie Brown, another student, had the initial idea and took it to Spiegel, who then invited Murphy to code the application. The trio, so the story goes, spent the summer of 2011 holed up in the Spiegel abode, creating what we now know as Snapchat.

Apparently, Brown was not an IT expert—in fact he was majoring in English—so while he was the person with the original idea, he did administrative tasks. His version of events is that he was forced out of the company, and as a consequence, he took legal action against Spiegel, Murphy, and the investors. This development parallels the fight over ownership of Facebook. Facebook founder Mark Zuckerberg was sued by a set of twin brothers who believed they contributed to the site's original idea, a legal case made famous in the Hollywood movie *The Social Network*. The brothers were eventually paid an undisclosed sum.

Fast-forward about ten years, and Zuckerberg nearly came to own Snapchat. He was mightily impressed with the app and made a bold cash bid to buy it. For the past few years, he has wanted to diversify Facebook as subscriber numbers decline, by buying a variety of apps and websites.

The fact that the owner of Facebook—the same owner who purchased Instagram for US$1 billion—was interested would be enough for any entrepreneur to sit up and take notice. When the cash purchase price offered was US$3 billion, you might think acceptance was a no brainer. Zuckerberg invited Spiegel to meet to discuss business, and Spiegel replied confidently, "I'm happy to meet you... if you come to me." In the end, however, Spiegel rejected the offer.

Yes, Spiegel rejected US$3 billion. That rejection may come back to haunt him, but at the moment some estimates place the value of Snapchat at around US$10 billion with a potential IPO at US$25 Billion. Clearly, he didn't want to jump at the first offer—a good piece of advice for budding entrepreneurs. Furthermore, this case shows that you wouldn't want to be playing poker against Evan Spiegel.

Let's look at some more lessons from Spiegel.

## THE BENEFITS OF EDUCATION

Spiegel can trace his skill at looking at things differently back to school. When only 15, Spiegel took extra classes at a local art school. One course on graphic design particularly appealed. Perhaps it was the strength of the teacher, but something clicked in the teenager's brain. Spiegel wrote that the "graphic design class took a hands-on approach to design thinking and was transformational for me as a student. I will never forget the typography experiments we completed during the course as well as the time spent in the letterpress lab."

Is it ever too late to tackle a new learning project? How much did an understanding of graphics and spatial design help Spiegel to imagine and create Snapchat? It's impossible to know for sure. But as an entrepreneur, one can always benefit from specific training and the acquisition of new skills. The success of young people in the technology business—all the way back to Bill Gates and Steve Jobs—comes from an understanding of new technologies and having new perspectives.

Some entrepreneurs in this book, like Alan Sugar, came from poor, even impoverished backgrounds. Spiegel wasn't one of them. He grew up in a world of privilege and wealth, and went to the best schools and colleges—his family home alone is worth millions.

Nobody recommends dropping out of school when you're close to graduation, but Spiegel had a good reason to leave Stanford University before getting his degree: He believed he had developed an app that could make him millions. He was wrong. Snapchat would make him billions.

## HUSTLE

Entrepreneurs of all ages typically have a strong desire to succeed in any way possible. As a teenager on a journalism project, Spiegel had to sell ads for a magazine, a task he relished. Are people born to be good at selling? No. While certain people have the personality or disposition to be great sellers because of their past environments or exposure, selling is a skill that can be learned. I know this first-hand from having trained hundreds of thousands of people how to sell, worldwide. But the will to sell, even if selling intimidates you, is what is most important. If you have the desire to be successful, then you need to will yourself to do all sorts of tasks that might initially make you uncomfortable, and do them well. Not only was Spiegel the most successful student at selling ads for the magazine, he also coached the other students to improve their selling techniques.

When studying at college, Spiegel was keen to work. He became an avid consumer of the beverage Red Bull. He enjoyed drinking the product so much that he was determined to work for the company. How did he go about getting a job there? "I found a friend who knew a guy that worked there, and I begged him for a job," Spiegel says. "I called him repeatedly, we met for coffee, and I agreed to do anything at all for Red Bull."

Do you have that kind of passion? If you have the passion, then does it drive you to succeed at any cost? In other words, how determined is your determination? On the other side of the equation, if someone comes to you looking for work, do you factor their enthusiasm and passion level into whether to hire them? If someone like Spiegel went to the trouble he did to get a job, would you hire that person?

Back to his days at Stanford, in a business-school class, Spiegel met Scott Cook, the founder of Intuit, a business-and tax-software company. He saw Cook's brilliance and begged him for a job. The operative word here is *begged*. There seems to be no limit to the passion for success.

Cook gave Spiegel a job working on a project called TxtWeb. This gave Spiegel knowledge and skills, as well as information and experience, by learning how to take online data and make it available via SMS to people in Third World countries who didn't have

access to broadband Internet. Spiegel's experie
expanded because he hustled to learn.

## IF AT FIRST YOU DON'T SUCCEED...

Spiegel's story may suggest that success is easy to come by, that it's instant in the Technology Age. But many a tech entrepreneur has become wildly successful or even moderately successful only after an initial project went belly up. Before Snapchat, Spiegel set up a website with some Stanford University chums. This was a guide for students and their parents to help them make a positive application to the college of their choice. Sounds promising. However, according to Spiegel, nobody, repeat nobody used the site—just Spiegel's parents. If ever the adage 'if at first you don't succeed try, try again' can be applied, then Evan Spiegel is the perfect example.

## THE FIVE ESSENTIAL INGREDIENTS

As a mentor, I always talk about these five essential ingredients you need to be a successful entrepreneur:

- Purpose
- Passion
- Perseverance
- People
- Profit.

You can't buy these five factors. Instead, they are freely available to any entrepreneur who genuinely wants to be successful. Are you sure about your purpose? Do you have a powerful passion to succeed? Will you persevere when times get tough? Do you have the right people on your side? Do you know your revenue models? What's your fresh angle?

You can answer the above questions to discover how suitable you are to succeed as an entrepreneur. If you are lacking in any one factor, then do something to change the situation. If you examine Spiegel's life, you can see how he has earned a big tick against each of these five.

## WHO CAN START A COMPANY?

Spiegel was once asked who can start a company, to which he replied, "If I can, then anyone can." Spiegel did have the advantages of a wealthy family and privileged upbringing. However, millions of young people grow up in a similar situation, but few have become billionaires like he has. So, what's the secret?

Having a great idea certainly helps, and Snapchat surely is that. But being brave is another characteristic. You don't need qualifications or money for self-belief —that's free. When Facebook made a US$3billion offer and Spiegel turned them down, that act took courage and self-confidence. If you have both of those, then you may be better able to succeed as an entrepreneur.

## FINAL THOUGHT

Whatever you may think of Evan Spiegel, you have to admire his ingenuity, boldness and courage. While most were sitting in front of the TV watching sports, Spiegel was out creating the next great user experience. Soon after Zuckerberg made his pitch for Snapchat, Spiegel gave his small collection of Snapchat employees a book about the art of warfare. He was prepared to fight for his beliefs and his business. How much easier would it have been to take the money and run? His self-belief and self-confidence must have been sky high.

At any age, entrepreneurs need to take risks and make calculated decisions. In Spiegel's case, it has been proven to be a masterstroke.

Hustling, being relentlessly determined, and knowing your worth would be how I'd sum it all up for Spiegel.

## 22

# THE SECRET CHAPTER

Sales rolling in, freedom rolling out

If you've ever worked with me, been to one of my events around the world (or even spent more than 30 minutes speaking to me!), you'll know that sales is one of my favourite things. A business can have quality products and services, and flawless marketing and branding, but if you or your staff can't sell, well then you won't have a business for long.

From an early age, I remember being perplexed by this idea that I had to sit next to someone, day in, day out, who made the exact same money as me every hour, despite them putting in half of the work with half the passion, and achieving only half of the result I did. I remember speaking to my mum about it (who was working in sales at the time) and she said, "Well, if you really want to control how much you earn, based on how hard you work and on your results, get into sales." From here I started the journey of working out this thing called sales; door-to-door, business-to-business, shopping malls, telesales—you name it, I did it. And I loved it.

In the early days, the only reason I survived some of the catastrophic stupid mistakes I made (like spending all of my capital in one of my first businesses on a piece of marketing that literally made us one sale of US$50 and sent the company to breaking point, or hiring the wrong staff member, who I was paying more than I had each month) was because I did years of learning how to sell everything to everyone. This meant I could dig (sell) myself out of any hole I fell into. I knew that if I had to, I could stop everything, pick up the phone, and make money. Which is something that, at times, I really had to do to just make rent. My ability to influence and persuade was what saved me from my early, poor business decisions.

This early training changed the game for me because I knew that if I could learn to influence and persuade people in life, from a straight sell through to an investment, I'd be able to get what I wanted in life, including the one word that encapsulates success for me—choice. I would have choice to do what I wanted, when I wanted, with whomever I wanted. Sales equalled choice, sales equalled freedom.

Can you improve your ability to sell, influence and persuade? Do you spend time and money sharpening one of the most important (if not *the* most important) skills of entrepreneurship?

Here's a little reward for making it to the end of this book. Visit aaronsansoni.com/thinklike, where

I've prepared some free sales training for you—a gift from me :)

Learn to sell, influence and persuade NOW.

## BUILD YOUR A.R.T.

The personal brand will be one of the most important marketing tools in the next decade. You can start and sell companies and their brands, but you can't run away from yours.

When profiling the best sellers and influencers in my earlier years, I started to notice that the top performers were the ones who had what I now call A.R.T. They won sales, they were sought out by people instead of having to chase them, and overall, they had a higher perceived value than others, and therefore, they commanded attention.

I took the time to break down what they did and synthesised that into what I'm proud to have now taught on four continents to hundreds of thousands of people –A.R.T.

### 'A' stands for Authority & Expertise.

Now more than ever before we are looking for authorities and experts in an uber-connected, information-rich, fast-paced world of uncertainty.

In every industry, including yours, we look for and turn to experts and authorities for the answers. Think about it—something happens on the news and the first person they wheel out is 'someone someone, PhD' or 'someone someone, expert in whatever' for commentary. They don't call just anyone—they find the expert in that field because after decades in the media they know that we, the people, pay attention to them. If they are an expert in that area, what they say therefore must be right and must be heard.

Now this is not to say you need to have a degree or PhD to be heard. I barely passed high school let alone have a degree, but I've become an expert in my field of sales and business because I've studied, learned, failed, succeeded and helped others to get incredible results because I immerse myself in this world almost 24/7. I'll research, write books (like this), speak at events, promote my brand and serve the entrepreneurial community.

Now more than ever before, as a society, we are looking for people who are authorities and experts in their field. After we type our symptoms for a rash into Google Doctor and it says to immediately cut off our arm from below the elbow, we don't go running for the saw. Instead we call the men and women in the white coats and say, "Hey doc, what do you think?" And then when they prescribe us medication that we don't know, in writing we can't read, and then we rush next door to the pharmacy and gobble up the pills like a mindless zombie! Why? Because they are the authority. And authority means trust.

So how do we do it? There are a bunch of ways to establish yourself as an authority or an expert in your field, and here are a few:

## Get a website

Your-name.com—go register it (once you have read this book cover to cover). That might seem super-obvious but it's really important this gets done ASAP.

You need a base—a place where you can establish your digital self, imprint your beliefs and talents and tell the world about them (as well as create profit through an online shop later down the track). A website is a place for content and engagement.

You can get one made on almost any budget. Of course, this will reflect on the overall outcome, and therefore on your brand's perceived value, so think about it wisely. When I started out, my first site was AUD$500 and they took nine months (it was supposed to be four weeks!), and I learned from there. It's a lot easier now to get a site done but if you're serious, get a company that will represent you online at the level you deserve (don't forget my team at manhattanmedia.com.au can help too, so ask them if you need a hand).

Lastly, on your website, start with the basics: good pictures of you and what you represent, and a blog where you can share your thoughts and engage your tribe.

## Social media

Social media is where you GIVE. It's where you let your tribe see your A.R.T.

Let me start with the biggest mistake—trying to do all social media platforms at once, especially when you're starting out. Depending on the typical age of your target market, I'd suggest different platforms. Here are some broad suggestions:

- Female 18-30: Instagram & Pinterest
- Male 18-30: Twitter & Instagram
- 30-60: Facebook.

Start by picking the biggest market that you want to focus on sharing your brand with, and that wants to hear from you. Once you finish learning the full A.R.T. here, you'll have a better idea of it.

Remember that your focus with social media is growing a brand through giving content, if you already have a market following you then use all the elements I mention here to strengthen their connection with you before you start creating your profit streams.

### Write a book/blogging

In the Information Age, where content is king, those who are creating it are seen as the experts. There are two key ways I'd suggest you do this: one, from your own experience, talking about how you are an expert in your area; and two, talking from another's point of view via interviews. It's a common misconception that you need to be a superhero in a field to have others see you as an expert, but there are many ways to grow your authority—not all great coaches are former players.

'A' stands for Authority & Media

This is an incredible vehicle for amplifying your influence and credibility. When I started out, my strategy was to write content and submit it, online and via post, to literally every magazine and newspaper I could find an address for. This still works, but now you can get PR agencies who have direct personal connections to the media to help with this exposure. The more you can be on TV, radio, print and online publications, the more trust and authority you will gain, which is a perfect segue into the next element of A.R.T.

'R' stands for Results & Proof

In a busy online world where every person and every brand is vying for a piece of our attention (and wallet), we need to create cut-through.

Statistics show that in just one day, from when we wake up in the morning to when we go to bed, we're marketed to more than 3000 times! This means that we need to create a personal brand that

stands out. One of the key ways to make this happen is by showing that your brand can deliver people results or help them get the results they're looking for. Just like in business, where a brand is a promise of delivery, you yourself as a personal brand are the same. Think about every job you've applied for —what are they really looking for? Past experience? Maybe. A degree? Sometimes. Knowledge and belief in their gut that you can definitely get the results required in the role? Absolutely.

In a world where everyone says, "I can do this", we're looking for the next level of certainty, and this comes from getting people to believe, without question, in the results that your personal brand can deliver.

Start by getting a few testimonials on video, or at least in writing (you'll need it for your website anyway), and keep a track of your successes in the area you're planning to grow your brand in.

The proof element of this is a deeper and even more important part of the equation. We have all heard, seen and read all kinds of proof, from 'I lost 40kg in just 30 days' to 'I made $10,000 from just one strategy'. Now these 'results' have their place—even I use them—but what's more powerful than a result, what connects with people more than a statement, now, in the 21st century, is proof.

Proof is the story behind the results. It's the human element that people pay attention to. You see, 50 years ago, even five years ago, you could simply show someone a statement that said, "I lost 40kg in 30 days", and POW! you had cut-through, and your customer, itching to shed those unwanted kilos, was listening and buying. However, because almost EVERYONE uses this in their marketing, it lost its pizzazz. So, what's more real to someone: that result, or learning that Jane lost 40kg in 30 days, found her inner confidence, is keeping up with the kids, no longer feels depressed, has a radiant smile, and the doctors say she'll live a longer healthier life? You tell me, what has more appeal and cut-through? Is it the direct result? Or is it the story behind the result, the proof, which makes it more real and believable? I'm guessing the proof. And better yet, the combination of result and proof that really wins.

## 'T' stands for Trust, Authenticity & Your Story

Yes, I squeezed a few things into this last letter, but they are all important ingredients of a successful personal brand. Trust is key. People need to know, trust and like you before they will listen and invest in you, your products and your company.

One of the vehicles of trust-creation is being authentic. This might sound simplistic enough, but it seems as we evolve we're becoming less 'ourselves' and more an 'idea' of what we think we should be. Now, it's key to present your image correctly, and I'm the first to admit that I think about my brand like this constantly, but I still remain standing in my truth. What that means is that I try to remain as open and honest and as attentive as possible with those around me. I share my life on a daily basis with hundreds of thousands of people live, and millions online. I share stories of my past, from a childhood of divorce, of lower-class and minimal opportunities, to my failures in business and life, to successes and gratitude. Giving others a chance to hear the REAL you is more liberating for you—and for them—than virtually anything else.

I still remember the moment I first shared my childhood on stage. I looked out at the arena of people who were busily jotting down strategy after strategy to grow their businesses, and I was talking about a recent success using the strategy, and everyone was loving the training. And I looked down and I saw a young guy, who would have been no more than 18. He looked deflated, which was uncommon for my event. I could instantly tell he felt that what I had achieved seemed impossible for him to do, it seemed that he couldn't ever get to that level; it was just an unattainable dream.

I asked the young man about his life. Turned out he grew up a few suburbs, away in the outer suburbs of Melbourne, like I did. He had a similar upbringing, without having much, and a life seemingly destined for mediocrity.

At this point I had said nothing, I just let him talk.

I walked over to my laptop and closed my slides. I opened a folder marked Old Pictures and found a photo from when I was about seven. I asked him what he thought of the picture and he instantly said, "It reminds me of where I grew up. It reminds me of my family." It was at that moment that I sat on the chair next to him, looked him in the eye, and said, "That was me; I'm still the same person, I'm not better or worse, I've just taken action and applied knowledge in my life to make a change, and stuck at it through the tough times. And in doing so I built a destiny by design and not default." He got it. Instantly he connected with the message and sat up in his chair with a smile. We both were almost in tears by the end of it.

Now this was remarkable, but what was totally

unexpected was, when I stood up and looked around the arena, every person was on the edge of their seat, engaged, many in tears or close to it, brimming with emotion.

Really? My story was just like a lot of people, why did they connect with it? It's at that moment that I decided to play full-out in my life, step into my truth, and share it to empower others by showing that there are choices and there are options for you in life, regardless of what your life is. You just need to decide to go for it.

What's your story? What's your truth?

I made something for you, FREE of charge on this very topic. To get your A.R.T. going, visit [aaronsansoni.com/thinklike](aaronsansoni.com/thinklike) and grab yours now.

## NAIVETY CAN BE YOUR BEST FRIEND

It may seem a somewhat counter-intuitive statement to make, that being naïve could help in the world of entrepreneurship, but what I found not only from studying people like those featured in this book, but also from my own life, is that remaining naive in my one single belief that I can really do/try/succeed at anything I want has served me well. It's lowered the resistance in my mind, the resistance that we all create at times, that we overthink things or suffer from 'analysis paralysis', or get gun-shy when the time is right to 'have a go'.

Remember when you were a kid and you'd climb that tree and then think, "What the hey, I'll just jump off, it's quicker and more fun than climbing down," and you jumped? Sometimes it hurt, and sometimes it didn't. Now you don't climb the tree, or if you do you hold on tight, and if you ever let the thought come into you mind about jumping, you probably follow it up with, "I wonder if the health insurance is up to date, just in case!"

Sure, naivety has lead me to fail a lot and in many ways, from wrong hires to failed businesses, to losing money and time. But on the other hand, it's allowed me to try a hell of a lot of things that I would have otherwise not tried, and some of those things have become my biggest success stories, from believing I could help others around the world, to running and investing in dozens of businesses that have become huge success stories.

So, the challenge here is to regain that inner kid; say yes more than no, have faith, jump, and always remember—you CAN do it.

## CASH COWS BUILD EMPIRES

Having travelled a good part of the globe and having spoken in front of literally tens of thousands of entrepreneurs, I'm often asked about how to grow an empire, not just one business.

This reminds me of the same question I was asking 15 years ago when I started my entrepreneurial journey. Unfortunately, I didn't get the answer I'm going to give you, so I made a few mistakes.

One of those mistakes was to make a little bit of money, get excited about my business success and go invest it all in every opportunity I could find. Two things happened: one, most didn't work out and drained me of all my money; and two, I took my eyes off the first business that made profit, and spent my time and energy chasing the 'new shiny thing'. As you can imagine, I was left with a lot of nothing and the prospect of starting again.

So here is the key—get the golden goose (or a few if you can) and look after it. Build the team of people to keep that ship sailing while you then start to test the waters on new ventures to build your empire, maybe even using the horizontal strategy I speak about in the next section. DON'T take your eyes off what's making you money right now—cash cows build empires, because they allow you to fail and still keep going if you manage the risk well.

Remember, a champagne fountain only works if champagne keeps pouring into the top glass.

## GO WIDE BEFORE DEEP

When building a business, whether it's your first or tenth, thinking of which way to build it is very important. Most businesses fall into what are called 'horizontal' or 'vertical' business structures.

A horizontal structure is a business that makes a cut of sales of their product or services by leveraging existing suppliers, contractors or businesses. Take your local supermarkets; most of them are horizontal structures. They don't make the food; they buy it from the manufacturer and wholesalers and on sell to us, the consumer. This means they don't make all the profits. They are middlemen. Some of the large chains now also manufacture foods so they can make a higher profit.

A horizontal structure is good at times, as it allows you to focus on selling a pre-existing product or service, and not be caught up with the actual delivery of what's promised.

Another example is an 'aggregator site' which is where several sources of information are searched to produce a result, such as a flights or hotels site like Expedia.com. They make money by comparing many products in the market for you, and ultimately getting you to make the booking through them and then charging the supplier for the service. They don't own the plane or the hotel.

The horizontal structure is a great way to lean on other established brands, products and services. This is a great strategy for an entrepreneur wanting to expand from one business to their second and third. Think about what customers you currently have in your business and what their needs are. What could you do to help them more? Said differently, what other products and services do they need besides yours, that complement what you offer? Take that information and find a business already offering these products or services (that doesn't compete with you) and set up a joint venture with them so you can sell their offering directly to your customers and pay them a share. This is different to a straight referral fee for passing a lead on; the other business offering becomes part of your own. This can be done in many different formats such as white labelling, which means putting your sticker over someone else's product and selling it, another great way to grow an empire and your brand.

Vertical structures are a little different and are usually higher reward from a profit standing, because you control things start to finish—you make and sell your products and services. Most typical businesses do this. Apple is a great example of a vertical business that completely owns the customer from hardware to software, manufacturing their own products, selling them in stores and online, and selling the software to run them, all the while creating a total eco-system for customers that means all profits end up at the same place.

Choosing a horizontal or vertical structure is really dependent on you and what business you want, and what stage you are at in your journey. There is an obvious advantage in vertical structures being more profitable, but along with that advantage comes more overhead costs, stock holding, capital and risk. Choose the one that suits you and remember that you can always start a horizontal business quickly and easily, and then turn it into a vertical as you grow and learn.

## PEOPLE

"Put your people first, customers second and shareholders third," said Sir Richard Branson, as he took the stage after me at a recent event that we headlined together in Australia. It wasn't the first time I'd heard him say it, but it reminded me again of this key piece of advice that I couldn't agree with more.

Build a loyal, hard-working team of 'believers'. It's critical to your entrepreneurial success. In addition to this you need to focus your time, energy and resources in the order Sir Richard has given. Why? Because a happy, productive team of engaged people will create happy, profitable customers. These happy, profitable customers will create happy, profitable shareholders. Which makes complete sense. The problems arise when entrepreneurs forget this process and focus on dollars only. Focus on your people; simple yet effective.

FINAL THOUGHT

Finding Obligation

I've purposely decided to finish this book on this note. In a book dedicated to helping you become a successful entrepreneur by learning from the successes of top business leaders, finding what I call 'obligation' will change everything.

I stared my journey like most, working for other people, some of whom appreciated me, some of whom didn't. I tried my own 'little adventures' and failed a fair amount before hitting a point when I started to seek out the mentors and leaders of the business world.

I received two types of advice, if I really break it down. One was business advice on systems, strategies and ideas to improve the business; the second was personal development advice. After all, as entrepreneurs we mostly go it alone in this world, caught up with our own imaginations.

The business advice varied, from what I've given you to what the 21 people in this book have spoken about, but the personal development advice seems to have always centred on the elusive 'why'. Why are you in business? What drives you?

I generally came up with the same answers as the person next to me: having something I'm proud of; for my family; having financial freedom; being my own boss. And so on.

These answers are what I now know as 'surface' reasons, and they really did drive me in the beginning. I would remind myself of what I wanted, I'd use it to keep myself focused, and I'd battle through the fears and doubts by grasping onto this idea that I had worked out what really drove me. I hit a few roadblocks along the way when I started to ask myself more questions, and stopped settling for the first responses I thought of: "I want to be financially free." Great, but why did I want this? "I want to have choice, and a big home and a nice car."

Again, I bought it for a little while, until I started to get those things that I had envisioned as the holy grail of achievements. I was grateful, absolutely, but I noticed that the way I was approaching my goals and life were 'me' based—even the ones around my family. Giving them things and changing their lives.

It took me years of learning, growing and teaching others to finally arrive at what I can now say is the single biggest concept that has kept me on fire and driven. Obligation.

On first hearing the word, some feel it has a negative connotation, like "I'm obliged to go see my in-laws", or "I feel obliged to show up to this event", but I believe this is what gives the word power.

To me, Obligation is the understanding that what I do, how I do it and why I do it at all, in its entirety, is not about me. Everything from going to the gym, to selling a product to someone, to being a father, to writing this book—it's all 100% about everyone else.

Take selling for example. Most have a fear about sales, stemming from this feeling that it's a cloak-and-dagger industry and that getting money from someone in exchange for your products is incongruent with your philosophy on why you got into your business. Since finding Obligation, I have found a new way to see this, a way that empowers me and helps more people than I ever could have imagined. You see, if I'm in a sales situation and I'm trying to sell any one of my company's offerings, I'm not focused on the money, or even my 'whys' being fulfilled. I'm focused entirely on helping the person in front of me to achieve what it is that they really want from this purchase as the knock-on effect. I'm focused on serving this person to the best of my abilities in order to help them achieve everything that they want. I'm focused on the Obligation I must make sure that the person in front of me, online, on the phone or in the boardroom says yes to acquiring the offer in front of them. Moving them away from pain, I move their lives to pleasure.

I'll give you an example. After some companies of mine started to do well, from tech to media and a few little ideas in between, people started to ask for my help with their businesses. This grew from "I'll chat with you for half an hour, just buy the coffee" to a huge educational business that has reached more than two million people in 18 counties, and counting. This didn't just happen because of marketing the brand and having good products—it happened because I realised early on that the only reason a person was in front of me or one of my team was to help them improve their business. They were there to change their lives, their own team's lives, their clients' lives, and everyone else who relied on them to be successful. They were there looking for help, and therefore no amount of reasons would allow my team or myself to let them go anywhere until we had helped them. We knew that our product was going to literally change their lives and businesses forever, put their children through the school of their choice, get them the home they wanted, help them help more of THEIR customers, all through selling our product to them and getting them to follow it.

It wasn't about price, it wasn't about time, it was about an unwavering feeling in our guts that we were Obligated to help them.

I'll never forget the day Garry came into the health club that I was running at the time. It was a Sunday and I was filling in for a sick team member. The day was quiet and only a few people were on the treadmills and in a class upstairs.

I got a call from reception that someone was there to be shown around; a 'walk-in', as we called it. I went out to the reception where I was greeted by a man in his late forties, overweight and looking like he needed hug.

We had a quick chat about his goals, why he wanted to join, and then I took him on a tour. I showed him the facilities and then we sat back down and I continued the sales process. I was well versed in it, as I had created most of it and trained the entire company. Garry said all the right things. He wanted to lose weight, he wanted to feel better, he was sick of being his size. To top it all off, his father had died at 48 years of age from a weight-related condition. Garry was larger than his late father, and in his mid-forties.

"Let me think about it," he said. "I have to speak to my wife about the price. I'll hold onto this and let you know".

I did everything to overcome Garry's objections, but he was not budging. It was a "Thanks for the tour and the coffee, but I'll think about it and get back to you."

Garry got up from his chair and headed to the door after a last-minute exchange of brochures and a handshake, and I started to head back to my office. I took two steps and stopped dead in my tracks. I suddenly realised something—Garry was in worse shape, in every possible way, than his father who had died. Garry was crying out for change but he had all the excuses. "Oh my God," I thought, "if Garry leaves I might be contributing in some way to his death by letting him carry on with his life, knowing all I know".

I turned just in time to see Garry grab the door handle and open it. "Stop!" I said (actually yelled), quite abruptly. Garry turned and looked at me from the half-opened door. "You're not going anywhere".

He looked a little stunned and confused. I turned to face him and took a few steps forward. "Garry, don't bullshit me. You want to change, don't you, and you're shit scared of dying like your dad did and leaving behind your beautiful family, but you know the road ahead to change is a hard one.

"Garry, how many times do you come into a gym, look around, and always find a reason to not join?"

"About once a year," Garry replied, with a look of authenticity and honesty I'll never forget.

"I'll pay. I'll pay your fees if you join today" I said.

"It's not the money, it's..." he replied, looking down.

I gestured for Garry to come and sit down again in the same seats. He did and after about 20 seconds, although it seemed like four hours, Garry looked at me and opened up.

We forgot for a moment that my 'job' was to sell Garry a gym membership, joining fee and, who knows, maybe even a backpack, a towel and multi-location access. We forgot about that and just talked about what had to change and why it had to change, and if it didn't what was really the repercussion.

Garry showed me a picture of his family; his wife and 10-year-old son. WHACK! It hit me again—if Garry leaves I'm affecting all of their lives by not doing my part and helping him change his life.

Garry talked about his work and how his business was suffering because he was tired and disinterested, and he may have to lay-off a team member who'd just signed a contract for her first home. WHACK! Again it hit me—he's going affect her and her family's life. The ripple just didn't stop.

I was now in total Obligation. I wasn't thinking about the sales goals of the business that month, or the commission cheque I'd receive, and I wasn't thinking about upselling Garry or anything else, other than this man must join today and must change now. He could see it in my face; he could feel it in my presence. Even I could feel it! Garry was not going anywhere. There was far too much riding on it for him.

Garry joined and lost a huge amount of weight. I called him every month to make sure he was on track. This became far more than just selling something, it was saving Garry's life. Business goals and sales had collided in a brilliant, amazing, life changing way.

I found Obligation that day and it's served me since, in all areas of my life. From selling something I believe in and that I believe will serve the person or company in front of me, to managing my team to achieve for their families and lives; from going to the gym to keep me healthy and fit and focused so I can get more out of my day, to being the best father, role model and husband I can be for my family, and showing my children a life of happiness, fulfilment and gratitude.

Now when I look at someone I see my Obligation to serve them and everyone that's relying on them, from an arena of thousands to a private client I'm working with one on one. Obligation will change the way you operate forever.

## ABOUT AARON SANSONI

**Aaron Sansoni** is the new breed of selling superstar: international speaker, bestselling author, recent nominee for EY Entrepreneur of the Year 2016 & Australian of the Year 2017.

Aaron's effected the lives of over 2 million people, in 41 countries in over 100 industries on and offline, through his training that spans a decade of mentoring.

Featured in over 20 publications around the world, Aaron runs a successful venture capital company with interests in media, tech, events, retail, and real estate projects around the globe.

Aaron is an internationally acclaimed speaker who has spoken at some of the most exclusive venues around the world and shared the stage with business icons including billionaire Sir Richard Branson, Hollywood A-lister Arnold Schwarzenegger & world-leading speakers such as Tony Robbins, Gary Vaynerchuk, Tim Ferriss and Dr Eric Thomas.

But where did it all start?

Growing up in a disadvantaged environment and a broken home in the outer suburbs in Melbourne, Australia, Aaron was one of seven children cramped under one roof. He spent most of his time playing basketball and thinking of inventions and business ideas that would change his life. In his early school years, he was told he had attention deficit disorder. His teachers constantly reminded him that he wouldn't amount to anything.

By age 9, Aaron was doing a regular paper round. By 12, he had started his first business, a local car-washing for neighbours. At age 16, Aaron realised his passion for sales and went on to work in everything from door-to-door, over the phone and face-to-face sales, achieving phenomenal results along the way. By the age of 23, he had amassed over a decade of sales experience, knowledge, training and world travel. Aaron opened his first consulting firm alongside his business empire, with the goal of helping business owners and entrepreneurs across the world realise their full potential, a goal he still has to this day.

Aaron now splits his time between running his hugely successful investment firm **Paragon Global Investments**, travelling the globe to educate business owners, sales professionals and entrepreneurs on how to build their own business empires. He is also a dedicated husband and a father to a son and a daughter.

Recently, Aaron has taken his philanthropic endeavours to a new level with the creation of **Aaron Sansoni Foundation**, a charity set up to help the underprivileged in Australia and abroad. This came about from year of personally donating to and helping raise awareness for other charities, including the Kathleen Keegal children's fund, two orphanages in Sri Lanka that care full-time for children orphaned after the 2004 tsunami. Aaron and the orphanage help in providing them a safe and loving environment.

Aaron is a mentor to top CEOs, athletes and celebrities and has personally helped his clients make billions of dollars in sales from his four award-winning global education brands.

aaronsansoni.com

*This book is dedicated to my beautiful daughter Alessandra, my wife Elena, and each and every entrepreneur out there working tirelessly to achieve what others around them THINK impossible. Yes, this book is dedicated to YOU! May it help you on your entrepreneurial journey to leave a mark on the world.*

First published in 2016
This edition published in 2016 by Manhattan Media, a division of
Paragon Global Investments Pty Ltd
Copyright © Aaron Sansoni 2016
The moral right of the author has been asserted.

All rights reserved. This publication (or any part of it) may not be
reproduced or transmitted, copied, stored, distributed or otherwise
made available by any person or entity (including Google, Amazon
or similar organizations), in any form (electronic, digital, optical,
mechanical) or by any means (photocopying, recording, scanning or
otherwise) without prior written permission from the author.

PO Box 1344, South Melbourne, Victoria, Australia, 3205

Although the author, his team and publisher have made every effort to ensure that the information in this book was correct at press time, the author, his team and publisher do not assume and hereby disclaim any liability to any party for any loss, damage, or disruption caused by errors or omissions, whether such errors or omissions result from negligence, accident, or any other cause. No part of this book may be reproduced or transferred in any form or by any means, graphic, electronic, or mechanical, including photocopying, recording, taping, or by any information-storage retrieval system, without the written permission of the author.

The accuracy and completeness of information provided herein and opinions stated herein are not guaranteed or warranted to produce any particular results, and the advice and strategies contained herein may not be suitable for every individual or business. All net worth references are via Forbes.com at time of publishing.

The author, Aaron Sansoni Group Pty Ltd and Paragon Global Investments Pty Ltd shall not be liable for any loss incurred as a consequence of the use and application, directly or indirectly, of any information presented in this work. This publication is designed to provide opinion regarding the subject matter covered. The author along with his team have made all efforts in the research of each person featured in this book. This book is sold with the understanding the author is not engaged in rendering legal, accounting, or other professional services. If legal advice or expert assistance is required, the services of a competent professional should be sought.